THE FRANCHISE

BOSTON RED SOX

A Curated History of the Sox

SEAN McADAM

Library of Congress Cataloging-in-Publication Data

Names: McAdam, Sean, author.
Title: Boston Red Sox : a curated history of the Sox / Sean McAdam.
Description: Chicago : Triumph Books, [2022] | Series: The franchise | Includes bibliographical references.
Identifiers: LCCN 2022010684 | ISBN 9781637270004 (cloth) | ISBN 9781637270370 (epub)
Subjects: LCSH: Boston Red Sox (Baseball team)—History. | Boston Red Sox (Baseball team)—Humor. | Boston Red Sox (Baseball team)—Miscellanea. | Baseball—Massachusetts—Boston—History.
Classification: LCC GV875.B62 M29 2022 | DDC 796.357092/274461—dc23
LC record available at https://lccn.loc.gov/2022010684

This book is available in quantity at special discounts for your group or organization. For further information, contact:

Triumph Books LLC
814 North Franklin Street
Chicago, Illinois 60610
(312) 337-0747
www.triumphbooks.com

Printed in U.S.A.
ISBN: 978-1-63727-000-4
Design by Preston Pisellini
Page production by Patricia Frey

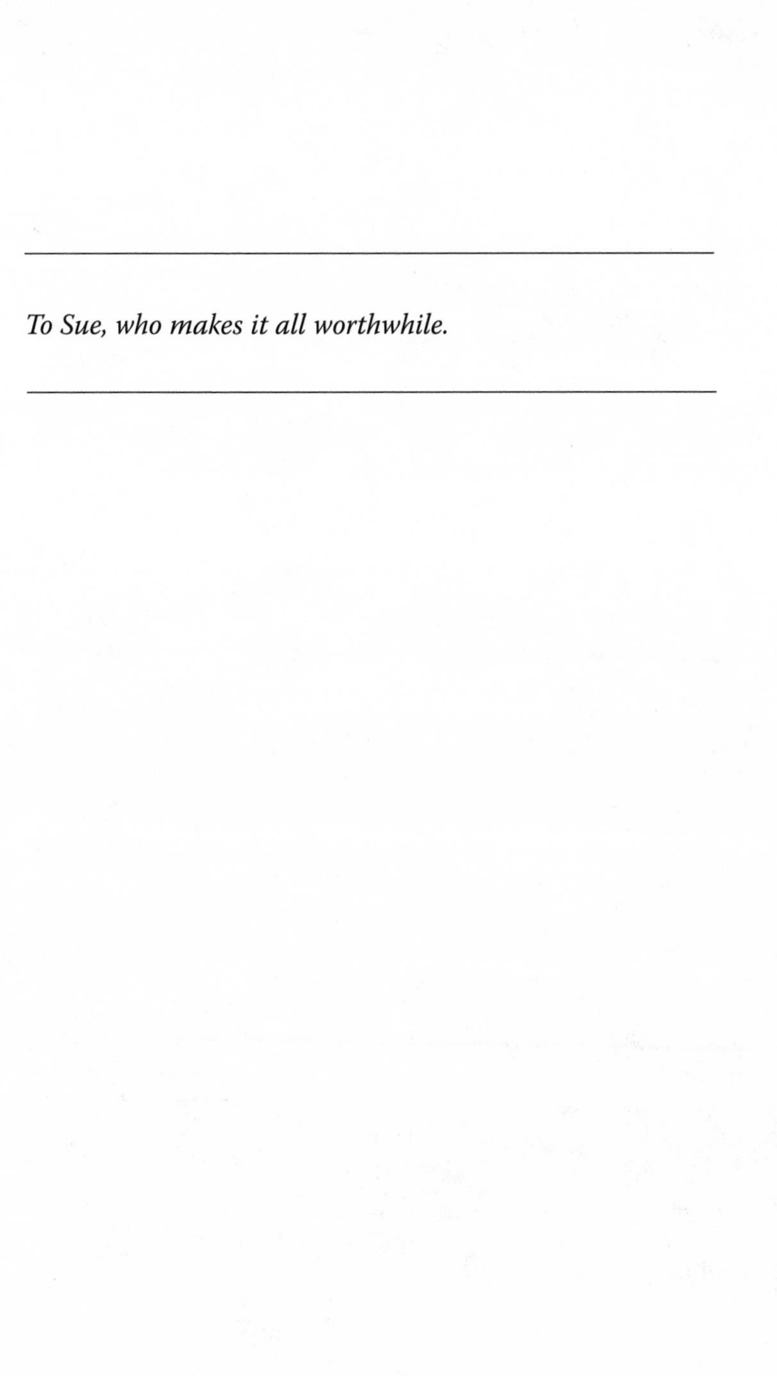

To Sue, who makes it all worthwhile.

CONTENTS

PART 4 The Icons

PART 5 The Aces

PART 6 Just Missed

PART 7 The Golden Age

Part 8 Transformative Figures

Foreword

Before I signed with the Red Sox in January 2003, all I knew about them was that they hadn't won a World Series for a long time. I never really followed the Red Sox or paid attention to any of the details until I got there. But I soon found out.

I saw how traditional the ballpark was, and when you start playing for the Red Sox, the history starts surrounding you and you get to know more about all the great players that played for the organization throughout the years.

The one thing that kind of hit me, after the first few months, was how fanatical everyone was. The type of fans the Red Sox had were different from the ones who followed other teams. They were obsessed with winning the World Series. My first year, when I first got there, we started winning and the fans started filling Fenway. It was the beginning of something special.

I had some big moments in that first season in Boston, but for the first few months, I wasn't even playing regularly. I remember getting a walk-off hit at Fenway against the Yankees, off Armando Benitez, and that was it. That's when everything started clicking for me.

The reaction to that hit was 100 percent different from anything else I had experienced in my career. That place got *loud,* and the fans went crazy. I remember that it was a day game, and afterward, I took my family to a restaurant. Everybody lined up to give me high fives. I don't think I had to pay for dinner, either; that was my first free pass!

When I got to the big leagues, everybody always mentioned Ted Williams—the last .400 hitter and everything. But once I got to the Red Sox, that was the whole talk. I looked into his career and the things he was able to do amazed me. I wish I could have met him. I got to meet so many of the Red Sox legends—Mr. Carl Yastrzemski; Jim Rice became like a father to me. Those guys were so special, and I have such respect for all those guys. They're legendary and it's an honor for me to have my name mentioned with them and to have my name up there at Fenway Park with theirs. To me, they're like superheroes.

I never looked at myself as one of those guys. When I joined the Red Sox, I had just been let go by the Minnesota Twins and I was out of a job. The Red Sox signed me and gave me the opportunity to play, and it was the best thing to happen to me in my career. In Boston, I really learned what my priorities were. Walking into the clubhouse, and looking at all the superstars that were there, I was like a sponge. I decided I was going to learn from every single player in that clubhouse. I wanted to know why Nomar Garciaparra was so good, why Manny Ramirez was so good, why Pedro Martinez was so good.

Every single one of them had a different approach, but at the same time, it was the same—hard work, dedication, and discipline. And I decided that I was going to focus on those things, too.

Those great stars who came before me—Williams, Yaz, Rice—never got to win a World Series; I won three. I guess I was the lucky one. Those guys did what they were supposed to. It just didn't click. Those guys, to me, were champions, even if they didn't accomplish what they wanted. As individuals, they accomplished a lot. But to win a World Series, you need 25 guys pulling in the same direction.

Especially after what happened to us in the 2003 postseason, the fans became so motivated. For so many years, they expected the worst—and I don't blame them. After 86 years without winning, what do you expect? And after the 2003 ALCS, I got it, too. I thought, *OK, playing here is ride or die.* I told myself, *You've got to get ready, son, if you want to survive in this jungle. This is a whole other level when you play for the Red Sox.*

For us, in October of 2004, everything clicked when no one expected it to happen. Making that comeback against the Yankees. That Yankees team was the most dangerous team I ever competed against in my career. That lineup was ridiculous and coming back to beat them, down 3–0, I never saw it coming. Even today, I sit down and watch the highlights of that series and to be honest with you, I still can't believe it happened. That was the most satisfaction ever.

The energy that you needed for those series...it wore you out. What prepared me to perform well in those kinds of series was playing winter ball in the Dominican. The pressure was similar and after playing all those years of winter ball, it helped me control my emotion in those big games down the road. I wanted to be part of those situations, those close games. Being able to come through in those spots, that was my thing.

The fans in Boston always gave me so much, and that was really true in 2016, my last year. I didn't expect that reaction. Whenever I came to the plate, I felt that love from them.

Even today, Boston and the Red Sox are in my blood. I can never stay away. Whenever I'm there, people always show me the love and tell me that they loved watching me play and how much they enjoyed my career. It's nice to know I was able to make so many people happy.

Being a member of the Red Sox organization was special, and it always will be.

David Ortiz
January 2022

Introduction

Like a lot of other baby boomers, my introduction to baseball and the Boston Red Sox came during the magical 1967 Impossible Dream season.

I was not quite eight years old when my dad first took me to Fenway. That first game was the day after Tony Conigliaro's beaning, and the Red Sox won, as Ned Martin probably described it, "a wild and woolly one" against the California Angels 12–11.

It was a typically thrilling game from the team nicknamed the Cardiac Kids, and I was hooked for good.

I remember plenty from that day—how incredibly green the grass was, how white the home uniforms were, how big even the game's smallest ballpark appeared. What I could not have imagined was that I would someday make my living chronicling the Red Sox for a living. As this is written, I've covered them for 33 years...and counting, or most of my "adult" life.

As a fan first, and later as a reporter, I've seen the Red Sox be everything from bad to great, including four championships and everything in between. They've been both confounding and compelling, but seldom have they been uninteresting.

The Red Sox have almost always meant something to their fans. They're not background noise in the summer, or an occasional pastime. That may apply elsewhere, where baseball is a leisurely pursuit, where going to a game is just one more entertainment option to consider. The Red Sox matter, and as someone charged with writing about them and talking about them, that deep-seated interest has served me (and my career) well, and I feel fortunate to work in a region with so much passion for the game and the team.

I know firsthand how much the Red Sox mean to people, because I experienced it—first as a young fan myself, and later, as a dad.

As a divorced father for about a decade, the job of covering baseball often took me away from home. But it also served as a lifeline to my daughter, Liza, and my son, Conor. In the early 2000s, when interest in the team was at an absolute apex, my kids became obsessed with the team, and my job provided us with one more connection, for which I will always be enormously grateful.

When I called them nightly, often from some baseball outpost, baseball served as one more connection for us. They were thrilled that I could provide them with inside updates, and I was thrilled there was one more thing over which we could bond. They visited me in spring training, got to meet some players, and were present at Yankee Stadium when the Red Sox beat the Yankees for the pennant in 2004.

Later, when I began dating my future wife, Sue, who had two daughters of her own—Amanda and Leah—one of the first times our soon-to-be-blended family gathered was to attend 2005 Opening Day, when the first championship flag for the franchise in 86 years was hoisted at Fenway. That remains a lasting memory for all of us.

INTRODUCTION

It's unavoidable, I suppose, that I find myself connecting personal events to the baseball calendar. I sometimes catch myself thinking, *Oh yes, that particular thing happened the same day that the Sox made that trade or lost that game in extra innings.* Red Sox seasons have become my own life's mile markers.

My work has taken me all over the United States, to the Caribbean, and, memorably, to Japan. Mostly, that's been rewarding, though at times, the usual hassles and inconveniences associated with business travel have made for some trips I would rather forget.

As anyone who has followed the game understands, there's a rhythm, a comfortable familiarity to each season. That's not to be confused with drudgery, or boredom, which I've seldom experienced. The old cliché really is true: every day, you see something at the ballpark that you've never seen before.

To date, I've seen thousands and thousands of games, been to many All-Star Games, and covered close to 20 World Series. I've waited in more hotel lobbies at the Winter Meetings than I'd care to count. I cannot say I've enjoyed all of it, but I can fairly say I've enjoyed most of it, and that's a good batting average for any job.

Over the years, the game on the field has changed and so, too, has the way it's covered. When I began, the internet didn't exist, but afternoon newspapers did. *That's* how long I've been doing this. But at bottom, the job remains the same—to tell the reader what happened and why.

When I first undertook this book, the task of presenting a curated history of a franchise that's been in existence for more than 120 years seemed more than a little daunting. I've mostly focused on the team's modern history, figuring if you want to know more about Babe Ruth or Jimmie Foxx, there are plenty of other books that can satisfy your curiosity.

I'm sure I've omitted things you thought were important. My wish is that I've also included some things you didn't know or offered a perspective you hadn't considered. If so, I've done my job and you've gotten something out of the process.

I hope you enjoy.

January 2022

PART 1

HISTORY

1

Fenway Park

In the annals of North American professional sports, it's doubtful that any athletic facility—ballpark, stadium, arena—was ever more strongly associated with its primary tenant than Fenway Park is with the Red Sox.

Built over several years and opened in 1912—famously, on the same day the Titanic sank, creating an easy punchline for Red Sox fans and foes alike—it has been the Red Sox's home for more than a century. (For some contrast, consider that the Texas Rangers, who didn't exist until 1971, are now occupying their third ballpark in Arlington, Texas.)

It is the oldest ballpark in Major League Baseball, older by two years than Wrigley Field—together the only remaining ballparks constructed before 1960.

There may be other ballparks as celebrated as Fenway, with Yankee Stadium being an obvious choice. But the House That Ruth Built, originally constructed in 1923, underwent major renovations in the mid-1970s and was closed for two full seasons before reopening in 1976. The original Yankee Stadium was then replaced in 2009.

Fenway—updated on occasion, gussied up particularly in the last two decades—still stands on the same footprint it occupied during World War I.

It's among the few MLB ballparks that have not succumbed to the scourge of title sponsors and corporate sponsorships. If the Red Sox ever were tempted to rename it in the mold of, say, Guaranteed Rate Field, it's likely the place might be burned to the ground by protesters before it could sport its new bought-and-paid-for branding.

Like its National League counterpart, its identity can be discerned with a single word. It's known—regionally, nationally, even internationally—as "Fenway." The "Park" part is optional, even a little unnecessary.

Its name comes from the neighborhood it inhabits, though it long ago surpassed the area of Boston after which it was named.

It has one of the game's smallest seating capacities, frustrating would-be ticket buyers when it comes time for the postseason or a special event like the 1999 All-Star Game.

For a while, that coziness was something of a handicap, as it precluded the Red Sox from selling another 10,000 or 20,000 additional seats and denying the franchise a chance to be on equal financial footing with those blessed with bigger capacities.

But in time, it came to represent part of its charm. And when the Great Ballpark Construction Revolution began in the early 1990s with the introduction of Baltimore's Camden Yards, teams began to opt for smaller—not larger—seating capacities.

Not only were smaller ballparks more aesthetically pleasing, suggesting a more welcoming environment, but offering fewer seats instead of more helped create demand. Fans couldn't decide to wait to buy tickets, knowing the inventory would always be available; instead, with fewer seats, an urgency was created as soon as tickets went on sale.

As new ballparks were built, there was a conscious movement away from the kind of antiseptic, multisport stadia built in the 1970s and 1980s, with the goal of constructing ballparks with more character. Some—including Minute Maid Park, *née* Enron Field—borrowed from Fenway liberally. Others did so in a more subtle manner, with asymmetrical dimensions and quirky design features.

Gone were the round, soulless facilities covered with artificial turf. Welcomed back were more modest-sized parks with some charm and soul.

Suddenly, Fenway didn't seem so anachronistic anymore. Like clothing styles that come and go in the world of fashion, Fenway had outlasted its contemporaries and eventually become hip again.

Twice in the last 60 years, however, Fenway's future seemed threatened. Both times, external forces combined to ensure its continued existence.

In the mid-1960s, with suburban growth driven by urban flight, Thomas A. Yawkey worried about Fenway's shelf life. Attendance had bottomed out—a reflection, as much as anything, on the noncompetitive teams fielded annually in the post-Williams era—and Yawkey undertook a study about moving the team outside the city limits, where parking would be more plentiful and land costs more affordable.

By the time he got around to pursuing it further, the 1967 Impossible Dream season reignited interest in the club and saw attendance surge again.

Then, in the late 1990s, with the team still owned by the Yawkey estate but effectively run by steward John Harrington, the club unveiled plans to replace Fenway by building a new ballpark around the existing one. Models were presented publicly.

It's not hard to understand Harrington's logic. At the time, the new ballpark boon was in full swing and baseball fans had found that "modern" didn't have to mean "sterile." Oriole Park at Camden Yards in Baltimore, in fact, was evidence that, with the proper planners and architects, a new ballpark could offer amenities like more legroom and spacious concourses without sacrificing charm.

Such was the affection for Fenway—peeling paint, poor drainage, outdated technology, and all—that the public blowback was swift and thunderous. And that was just the opposition from the fan base.

Soon, it became clear that some of the surrounding land needed for the new ballpark could not be acquired, as Harrington had hoped, by eminent domain. Then came resistance from public-interest groups, who questioned the wisdom of the project.

Still, Fenway's future wasn't ensured until the Henry-Werner ownership group won the bidding in late 2001. That group was the lone interested buyer committed to preserving Fenway.

"We felt very strongly that the facility could be saved and revived," said onetime club president Larry Lucchino.

At a price tag of more than $1 billion, over a series of upgrades and renovations, it was.

Folded into a neighborhood that was once residential, and bereft of adequate parking, it's easy to miss Fenway Park from a few blocks away. Though it occupies several blocks, it can sneak up on you if you're approaching it from a certain angle.

And then, suddenly, it's there, shoehorned into an area just a few blocks up from Kenmore Square and Boston University in one direction, and from the Longwood Medical area in another.

For all its charm and quaintness, Fenway sometimes was as much a curse as it was a blessing when it came to a competitive advantage for the Red Sox.

Undoubtedly, the ballpark's cozy dimensions helped the Sox offensively. The nearby Green Monster proved an inviting target for righthanded power hitters, who must have felt that they could almost reach out and touch the wall from the batter's box.

But too often, management constructed a team built for Fenway, managing to somehow forget that the team was required to play half of its games elsewhere, where Fenway's dimensions were not replicated and the club's personnel were ill-suited for bigger ballparks or ones that weren't as hospitable for righty pull hitters.

Moreover, the Sox historically became so enamored with hitting the ball off—and over—The Wall that they almost completely ignored pitching.

One thing that often surprises Fenway first-time visitors—opposing players, visiting writers or broadcasters, out-of-town fans—is the sightlines from many of the seats.

Viewed empty, with the seats bereft of fans, it's astounding to note how few of them are properly positioned.

The center field bleacher seats are oddly tilted not to the playing field, but to the seats in right field. At the same time, the seats in the right field grandstand are aimed at center field, and not the infield diamond, as might be expected.

On the third base side, the seats are positioned as to make it impossible to view balls hit into the left field corner. Similarly, fans in right are unable to follow play near the right field foul pole. (This was made obvious when Red Sox outfielder Tom Brunansky made a diving catch for the final out in the final regular season game in 1990, a play that virtually nobody seated on the first base side could possibly claim to have witnessed. Even the television replays at the time proved inconclusive.)

Direct sightlines aren't the only thing missing from the Fenway experience—so, too, is comfort.

While the Red Sox replaced lower-bowl box seats with (somewhat) roomier box seats, affording a bit more leg room, the cramped grandstand seats—most of them wooden and painted navy blue—are undeniably tight.

That's the price paid for sitting in a ballpark constructed more than a century ago. At the time, the average American male—and they were almost all males—stood nearly two inches shorter than in 2021. Anyone standing taller risks constant bumping of the knees against the row in front, and egress from the rows—many a dozen or so seats wide—is almost impossible without everyone standing to allow passersby to exit.

Of course, what Fenway may lack in modern amenities and creature comforts, it makes up for in atmosphere and energy.

Precisely because patrons are nearly on top of one another, the ballpark emits a volume of fan support that can be unmatched in ballparks with a seating capacity 10,000 greater than Fenway. And without multiple levels to accommodate stacks of luxury boxes, as is often the case in modern stadia, it can sometimes feel as though a sellout crowd is on top of the playing field, heightening the impact of fan reaction.

"Home-field advantage," said manager Alex Cora, "is real at Fenway. We love playing here in front of our fans. And when they get loud, you can feel it on the field."

* * *

Part of Fenway's charms are its unique attributes. It's the oldest and one of the smallest Major League Baseball ballparks, and that itself separates it from the pack.

But there's more than its physical appearance that gives Fenway its appeal. There are also its traditions.

Each year in mid-April—traditionally, the third Monday of the month—Massachusetts (and Maine) celebrates Patriots' Day, in recognition of the first battles of the Revolutionary War.

Schools are closed in Massachusetts, and the Boston Marathon, the country's longest-running road race, is held. Not incidentally, the Red Sox host a game at Fenway that begins at the untraditional baseball hour of 11:05 AM.

The first Patriots' Day game was held in 1903, three years into the franchise's existence. Not long after, the Boston Braves, the National League club in town, copied the idea, with an afternoon game of their own.

By the early 1940s, the teams reached a compromise, so as not to compete with one another: the Red Sox would be the host team on the holiday in even-numbered years, with the Braves doing so in odd-numbered seasons.

That back-and-forth continued until after the 1952 season, when the Braves, tired of being the city's second team, moved to Milwaukee.

Ever since, the Red Sox have seen to it that the schedule-makers have them home for Patriots Day, with the Sox and a visiting club finishing a four-game, wraparound series with the late-morning start.

The idea was to find a way to blend the two events—matinee baseball and the marathon—and allow sports fans to enjoy both. Fans leaving Fenway after the game could stroll down to Kenmore Square and watch the race leaders approach the final mile of their journey from Hopkinton.

But in 2013, the twinning of the two events took a dark turn.

The Red Sox had just finished a 3–2 walk-off win over the Tampa Bay Rays and were readying a bus to Logan Airport for a brief road trip to Cleveland when sirens cut through an otherwise glorious spring afternoon.

The sound of police sirens was not, initially, enough to cause concern. On a typical Patriots' Day, tens of thousands of baseball fans and race onlookers require heightened security and extra police presence. The sirens could have been responding to a traffic issue or a minor fender-bender.

But soon, the sirens multiplied, and so did the ominous feeling that something more troubling was underway.

No one, however, could have predicted the horror that had only recently unfolded near the finish line on Boylston Street: terrorists detonated two explosive devices, injuring many and killing three.

The attack consumed the Boston area for days, eventually resulting in a shelter-in-place order and a door-to-door search for the one of the terrorists in nearby Watertown.

The next night in Cleveland, Red Sox equipment manager Tom McLaughlin hung a jersey in the visitors' dugout that read BOSTON STRONG.

Four days later, after having the first game of the next homestand postponed with the city on lockdown, the Red Sox returned to play. A defiant David Ortiz declared, "This is our fucking city, and no one is going to dictate our freedom."

In an afternoon choking with emotion, the Red Sox managed yet another dramatic victory, achieved with an eighth inning, come-from-behind homer by Daniel Nava.

For the rest of 2013, the Red Sox seemed to bond, united in their determination to overcome the horrific events of Patriots' Day, while serving as a unifying force for the region.

That emotion seemed to carry the Sox all the way to a World Series triumph that October, the franchise's third title in the span of 10 years. Never was a championship so uplifting and healing.

* * *

Of all the defining characteristics of Fenway, nothing quite matches the ballpark's looming left field wall.

Known to many as the Green Monster for its sea-green paneling and its imposing 37-foot-high size, it is impossible to miss or mistake.

For most of its existence, it sat beneath a screen across its breadth, extending from the left field foul pole to the center field bleachers.

Home runs swatted over the structure would nestle gently into the netting, which reclined at an angle, hanging over Lansdowne Street like a hammock. Hitters took aim at the screen like a target in batting practice, with the most prodigious clouts clearing the structure altogether and scattering onlookers below.

The next day, ballpark workers would scale the ladder affixed to the wall and collect the balls collected the previous day. And then the assault on the wall would start all over again.

Of course, while hitters have long taken aim at The Wall, there is the other aspect of it: *playing* the wall. When Carl Yastrzemski wasn't utilizing the occasional inside-out swing to pepper balls high off the wall, he was busy patrolling left field in front of it.

In his career, Yastrzemski played thousands of games in left at Fenway and came to know it as few others. He knew its dead spots, its rivets, and its dents; as important, he knew what that would mean for the trajectory of the ball.

At times, the difficulty of playing the wall would get overstated. In one sense, it was a simple chore with a basic truth: as a left fielder in Fenway, any ball hit over your head was either leaving the ballpark altogether or coming back to you.

Ah, but Yastrzemski understood better than most just how and where the ball was ricocheting. Like an expert pool player, Yaz came to know the caroms and what they would mean for his pursuit. Few ever mastered the knack for retrieving the ball with one hand the way Yastrzemski did.

This was an exercise in efficiency. If Yaz could catch the ball barehanded, that would eliminate the split-second of time needed to transfer the ball from his glove to his throwing hand. And that split-second could sometimes make the difference between a baserunner being tagged out for his greediness at second base…or rewarded for his daring with a double.

Yastrzemski came to understand the wall so well that he became an expert at judging whether it would contain a well-struck ball. For those he deemed unplayable, Yastrzemski would barely budge, sometimes conveying the sad news to his teammates that the ball in question was indeed not coming back.

He became something of a human weathervane: if Yastrzemski refused to so much as turn around to track the ball in flight, sometimes failing to lift his hands from his knees—his pre-pitch setup—it was a clear signal that trouble was in hand. This could enrage pitchers, who deemed his stillness a sign of disrespect.

For Yastrzemski, it was a conservation of energy, and occasionally, just maybe, a message to his pitcher that a mistake had been made. *Make a better pitch, and perhaps next time, I'll be able to make a play.*

As part of makeover Fenway underwent under the John Henry ownership, the netting above the wall was removed in

2003 and replaced by three rows of seats, termed, logically enough, "Monster Seats."

The fan perspective is a unique one: ticket holders sit atop a famed structure, in the game's most historic ballpark, and have an opportunity to snare home run balls.

Occasionally, broadcasters have done their broadcasts from the Monster Seats, affording them the opportunity to see the game as fans would.

The Red Sox pitched these seats as a unique ballpark experience. The more cynical dismissed them as merely overpriced bleacher seats.

But aesthetics aside, the changes made to Fenway were significant and helped improve the fan experience. Concourses were widened, allowing for greater passage prior to, during, and after games.

In a nod to younger fans who might not hang on every pitch but instead view the idea of going to a ballgame as a social event as much as spectator sport, a right field pavilion that offered expanded beer choices and encouraged milling around proved popular.

Over the years, Fenway has hosted nearly every sport imaginable.

The ballpark was home to the Boston Redskins of the NFL from 1933 to 1936, the Boston Yanks in the 1940s, and later, the nomadic AFL Patriots from 1963 to 1968. The National League entrant in the MLB, the Braves, spent the 1914 and 1915 seasons there.

More recently, under the Henry-Werner ownership group, the ballpark has hosted high school football games, soccer matches, college hockey, and a Winter Classic NHL game between the Bruins and Philadelphia Flyers.

Beginning in the early 2000s, it also became a popular concert venue, with the Rolling Stones, Bruce Springsteen and the E Street Band, and Paul McCartney among repeat headliners.

But, more than a century old and deemed structurally sound for another few decades, Fenway remains, primarily, a baseball cathedral, home to one of the game's longest-running franchises, steeped in tradition but capable of charming newcomers on a daily basis.

SPRING TRAINING

Part of the charm that accompanies each baseball season is not knowing when—or where—it will end. In 2004, for instance, few could have imagined that that Red Sox season would conclude in St. Louis, with the Red Sox hoisting the World Series trophy.

But everyone knows when and where each season begins—in spring training.

No other sport enjoys a preseason like baseball. No other sport prepares for its regular season by moving its entire operation thousands of miles from its usual home. No other sport has as long a ramp-up with its preseason.

And certainly, no other sport can boast that its prep time also signals the beginning of the end of winter and the arrival of spring.

Football gets underway in the heat and humidity of late summer, anticipating the arrival of fall. Basketball and hockey get started in the fall, with winter on the near horizon.

Not baseball. It may be a cliché, but baseball promises a rebirth and renewal each February, a promise that better days (and warmer temperatures) aren't far away. No other sport so perfectly synchronizes its start to the rhythm of the calendar and the change of seasons.

Merely hearing the phrase "pitchers and catchers" is, for some, enough to take the chill off a cold January evening.

For most of their first half-century of existence, the Red Sox were a peripatetic bunch when it came to spring training. Over the years, they based camp in (deep breath): Virginia, Georgia, Arkansas, California, Florida, Texas, Louisiana, Maryland, and New Jersey. One year, during World War II, they trained at Tufts University, mere miles from Fenway.

But for most of their modern history, the Sox have decamped in either Florida or Arizona, the two states most closely associated with spring training.

From 1946 through 1958, they were situated in Sarasota, Florida. For a stretch of seven years, they headed west to Scottsdale, Arizona. Having decided that the Southwest wasn't very convenient for New Englanders wishing to get a sneak peek at the team, they returned to Florida in 1966, where they have trained ever since.

The Sox called Winter Haven home from 1966 through 1992. Winter Haven is situated some 50 miles southwest of Orlando in landlocked central Florida. An otherwise quiet, rural burg, it was once best known for its proximity to the tourist attraction of Cypress Gardens until the Sox established their preseason home and became synonymous with "The Have."

For more than a quarter-century, snowbirds from New England traveled to Winter Haven to get a break from freezing temperatures. They weren't difficult to spot with their pasty skin covered in zinc oxide.

The informality of spring training invites close contact with the players—or at least, closer contact than during the regular season. Smaller ballparks, less zealous security forces, and the absence of pressure combine to make players more accessible for autographs and general fan interaction.

It was not uncommon for fans to mingle with players in local restaurants and bars, or even poolside at the Holiday Inn.

To be sure, Winter Haven was not as pleasant an experience for some as it was for others. Even during the team's final years there in the late 1980 and early 1990s, the local chapter of the Ku Klux Klan was active, creating a hostile environment for players of color.

The Red Sox themselves did not help matters when, during the 1980s, they allowed the local Elks to distribute complimentary guest passes to their white players—and only white players—for their still-segregated club. Tommy Harper, who had played for the Sox in the 1970s and then served on the coaching staff, launched a discrimination suit against the team.

Every spring seemed to offer its own bizarre developments. After reporting late to spring training in 1991, Roger Clemens donned a pair of headphones and ignored new manager Butch Hobson, who jogged beside him in a futile attempt to establish a bond with his ace. Dennis "Oil Can" Boyd was found to be in possession of a stack of overdue adult movie rentals from a local establishment, leading someone to suggest he had been hosting his own "Can Film

Festival." Wade Boggs once tumbled out of a Jeep, angrily driven by Debbie Boggs, as it left a restaurant parking lot, leading one wise guy (OK, me) to note that the third baseman had "survived another falling-out with his wife."

You name it, and it happened in Winter Haven, and often in front of nearby fans. Once, pitching coach Bill Fischer, puzzled by reliever Lee Smith's decision to eschew the ninth inning as had been planned, chased after the closer as he headed for the Chain O'Lakes clubhouse, all the while bellowing, "Lee, Lee...what the fuck?" in front of mortified parents scurrying to cover their kids' ears.

In 1993, unhappy with outdated facilities in Winter Haven and eager to take advantage of the many municipalities offering to build them a new state-of-the-art spring home—being the home of a major league baseball team for some six weeks can be hugely profitable for cities and towns in Florida and Arizona—the Sox moved stakes to southwest Florida and Fort Myers.

They spent 20 seasons at City of Palms Park, near to downtown Fort Myers. The new ballpark was a modern marvel compared to its predecessor in Winter Haven, complete with luxury suites, increased seating capacity, and vastly bigger clubhouses and training facilities. At the height of the Red Sox–Yankees rivalry from 2003 to 2005, fans would sleep out on the sidewalk near the box office in the hope of snagging standing-room tickets for Grapefruit League meetings between the clubs—and never mind that only a handful of Yankees regulars would make the trek from Tampa, or that, as is tradition, many of the Sox stars would be out of the game by the sixth inning.

But a lack of available land in the area meant that the team's minor leaguers trained several miles down the road from the main facility, making for a lack of cohesion.

That was rectified in 2012, when the Sox moved into an unincorporated area of Lee County, on the outskirts of Fort Myers. Fenway South houses JetBlue Park, which features the exact dimensions of the actual Fenway, right down to a replica of the Green Monster in left field—the better to prepare newcomers to the organization for 81 games in Boston.

The new complex also featured a half-dozen fields behind the main ballpark, more than enough to host the team's minor leaguers, along with various other organizational endeavors such as extended spring training—for players rehabbing from injury—and the team's Instructional League program in the fall, and during the summer, it serves as host for the team's affiliate in the Florida Complex League (FCL).

Spring training can also be a cross-generational melting pot, with former stars—including Carl Yastrzemski, Dwight Evans, Luis Tiant, and Pedro Martinez—mentoring prospects, providing instruction on the game's finer points.

Ultimately, spring training is an opportunity for players to physically ready themselves for the demands of the upcoming season. That remains its principal objective.

But it also doubles as a delightful preview of coming attractions for shivering fans, anticipating the return of the summer game, to say nothing of summer itself.

2
The Yawkey Era

The legacy of Thomas A. Yawkey is impossibly complicated.

As the owner of the Red Sox from 1933 to his death in 1976—his family trust would own the franchise for another quarter of a century—Yawkey wanted nothing more than to see his team win championships, though they never did under his stewardship.

Yawkey spent lavishly on player salaries, formed close bonds with his star players, and grew to view his biggest stars as the children he never had. And yet, his tenure was marked by long stretches in which his ballclub was noncompetitive.

He oversaw the growth of Fenway Park and watched as it grew into a ballpark treasure, romanticized by novelist John Updike as a "lyric little bandbox," but in the mid-1960s, frustrated by the team's sagging attendance, he eagerly explored a move to the suburbs. Only the 1967 Impossible Dream season and the interest it spurred saved the ballpark from abandonment.

He earned a reputation as a benevolent owner, who enjoyed occasional forays into the clubhouse to mingle with players, even engaging in games of pepper with them. He was known to inquire about the well-being of players and their families and provide counsel and financial help to those who were struggling. Some Black players, including Reggie Smith, have shared stories of Yawkey's generous nature and genuine interest in their off-field lives.

And yet, Yawkey's Red Sox were the very last Major League Baseball team to integrate, adding a Black player even after the crosstown NHL Bruins. Stories—anecdotal and otherwise—abound about the team's indifference—if not outright hostility toward—Black talent, an approach that undoubtedly contributed to the team's endless championship drought.

Even if Yawkey himself was not racist—as, to be fair, some who knew him well vehemently claim—then he was guilty, at a minimum, of employing racists and turning a blind eye toward their prejudices.

As suggested: it's complicated.

* * *

Yawkey, in so many ways, came from a different era of sports ownership.

When Yawkey bought the Sox in 1933, the sports world wasn't full of entrepreneurs like Mark Cuban or tech executives like Steve Ballmer. There were no frustrated former college athletes, like Jerry Jones, who owned teams in a desperate bid to win vicariously through their employees. There were no litigious attorneys like Peter Angelos.

No, Yawkey had earned his money the old-fashioned way: he inherited it, mostly from his mother's family. Orphaned at 15, he was adopted by his mother's brother. At 16, a year later, Yawkey inherited $20 million as part of two trusts.

Throughout his life, Yawkey was often identified as a "sportsman," a designation that, today, seems hopelessly outdated. But such was the title given to wealthy individuals—industrialists, scions—who regarded their teams as expensive playthings and their investments as little more than hobbies.

Casual as they might have been, often their business interests were lifelong. Yawkey's family ownership lasted almost exactly 70 years, a length that seems impossible to imagine today. The closest comparison to his decades-long stewardship would be a number of longtime NFL franchises. The Pittsburgh Steelers have been owned since their inception by the Rooney family, and the same can be said of the New York Giants and the Maras.

But with no children to pass on the Red Sox—a highly valuable family heirloom—to, the Yawkey Trust auctioned off the Sox in late 2001. Three years later, in an almost cruel blow to the Yawkey legacy, the team ended its 86-year title drought.

To illustrate the sheer scope and duration of Yawkey ownership, consider that it began seven years prior to Ted Williams' big-league debut and lasted nearly 20 years after the retirement of his successor in left field, Carl Yastrzemski.

* * *

The arrival of Jackie Robinson to the Brooklyn Dodgers in 1947 helped baseball break its color barrier. Robinson was named National League Rookie of the Year and went on to a Hall of Fame career. In the months and years that followed—Larry Doby integrated the American League by debuting with

Cleveland only a few months later—many teams introduced Black players to their roster.

In fact, it would be difficult to tell the story of baseball during the 1950s without recounting the contributions of so many prominent Black players,

The Red Sox, at the very least, were not proactive in acquiring Black ballplayers. A handful of African American players were part of the team's minor league system, but none was a part of the major league roster until 1959, some dozen years after Robinson's historic debut. Even then, the introduction of infielder Pumpsie Green was seen at the time as a response to a threatened lawsuit more than a philosophic reckoning.

But the Red Sox's tangled racial history doesn't begin with Robinson's historic feat. Indeed, it predates that by several years, and ironically, includes Robinson himself.

In 1945, Robinson, outfielder Sam Jethroe, and Marvin Williams were invited to an amateur tryout at Fenway. While this was taking place, a voice from a nonuniformed member of the Red Sox was heard to exclaim, "Get those n—— off the field!"

To this day, there remains much conjecture as to who uttered the ugly slur. Some of Yawkey's defenders have maintained that records prove that he was not in Boston on that day. But whoever uttered the order was a member of the team's inner circle, and fairly or not, was interpreted as speaking for the organization.

Again, if Yawkey himself didn't say it—and there's no concrete evidence suggesting otherwise—at the very least, he was guilty of employing someone who did.

(Robinson, for his part, would later famously label Yawkey "one of the most bigoted men in baseball.")

Others, it should be noted, were quick to suggest otherwise. Reggie Smith, who spent parts of eight seasons in the Red Sox outfield and four more years in their minor league system, said on more than one occasion that he never saw any evidence of racism from Yawkey.

"Tom Yawkey treated me very fairly," Smith told the *Boston Glob*e in 2018. "I had conversations with him about the reputation that he had, and the Red Sox had during the time I was there. He wanted to make sure that he had a good team, and he wanted the best players he could possibly get. I was treated very fairly, and I know that when I left Boston, I was the highest-paid African American player that he had, and I respect him for it."

Smith was not one to tiptoe around the issue of race. He spoke of his experience in Boston candidly and told author Howard Bryant that he "never felt welcome in Boston." In Bryant's 2002 book *Shut Out: A Story of Race and Baseball in Boston,* Smith labeled the city racist.

Others were far less sanguine on the topic of Yawkey.

Tommy Harper played for the Red Sox for three seasons in the 1970s, and after his playing career ended, was a coach and consultant with the organization. Harper also brought suit against the team for allowing the segregated Elks Club in Winter Haven, Florida, the team's spring training home for more than 25 seasons, to provide guest passes to white players while excluding Black players.

"You can tell me all you want about philanthropy," Harper told the *Boston Globe.* "But don't tell me that in 1950, they were trying [to integrate the team]. You can't pick and choose. History is what it is. Does philanthropy outweigh the harm to African American players? Does it? It my opinion, it does not.

"I did not know Mr. Yawkey. The man was invisible. If you say that you know him and you know him as not being a bigot or racist, I have to accept your word. I don't know. That's why I stay away from calling anybody a racist because I don't know.... I can only go by policy, whether it's written or unwritten. I can only go by what I know, the history. Does that outweigh the philanthropy?

"What I'm saying is that you cannot say it was benign neglect, that Mr. Yawkey was never around. The responsibility goes to the ownership. Whatever happens at Fenway Park eventually winds up at the owner."

In that regard, it's difficult not to conclude that, at the very least, Yawkey was guilty of looking the other way on far too many incidents and practices during the course of his ownership.

* * *

Toward the end of his life, Yawkey, growing more desperate to win the title that had eluded him for decades, became more aggressive in his pursuit.

Even before free agency dawned on Major League Baseball, he greenlighted a deal that purchased outfielder Joe Rudi and reliever Rollie Fingers from the Oakland A's. The A's penurious owner, Charles O. Finley, anticipating a sharp uptick in player salaries with the advent of free agency, held a fire sale for his star players who had helped the franchise to three straight pennants from 1972 to 1974.

Finley sold Rudi and Fingers to the Red Sox and Vida Blue to the New York Yankees, but within two days, commissioner Bowie Kuhn voided both deals, invoking the "best interests of the game" clause that gave him such power.

(Historians have often wondered what would have happened had any of the players actually appeared in games for their new teams. Had this been the case, it might well have been harder—if not impossible—for Kuhn to intercede and negate the trades. Instead, the three players dutifully returned to Oakland and the Red Sox and Yankees were left to wonder: What if...?)

Yawkey's death in the summer of 1976, coming just months after the Sox lost to the Cincinnati Reds in the classic 1975 World Series, served as the end of an era for the franchise.

His widow, Jean, remained principal owner in the interim. It was her intention to sell the club to Haywood Sullivan—a former journeyman catcher and longtime favorite of her late husband—and Buddy LeRoux, who parlayed a long career as trainer for the Sox, Bruins, and Celtics into success in real estate and emerged moderately wealthy.

When fellow owners rejected the Sullivan-LeRoux bid as inadequately funded, Jean Yawkey became a partner, offering Fenway Park as collateral.

LeRoux and Sullivan, however, were ill-equipped—financially and otherwise—to be owners. Both essentially refused to acknowledge the advent of free agency, insisting on fiscal prudence. Sullivan, who had appointed himself as general manager and head of baseball operations, bungled contract talks with stars Rick Burleson, Fred Lynn, and Carlton Fisk, trading the former two while missing a contract tender date with the latter, freeing him from the team and enabling him to sign with the Chicago White Sox.

That three homegrown All-Stars would be treated so cavalierly by their original franchise was, predictably, not well received by the fan base. It was hardly surprising that the exodus of talent negatively impacted the on-field product. From

1980 through 1985, the Sox never finished higher than third in their division.

Worse, a nasty power struggle ensued between Sullivan and LeRoux, culminating in one of the most embarrassing spectacles in modern club history.

On the very night that the team was honoring former star outfielder Tony Conigliaro, who had suffered a near-fatal medical event a few years earlier, LeRoux decided to hold a press conference, anointing himself the true owner of the team while effectively firing Sullivan from his position as president of baseball operations. The effort was immediately branded the "Coup LeRoux."

A year of legal battles ensued, with the Sullivan-Yawkey side emerging victorious. Still, the squabbling took its toll on the team's brand and the on-field product.

Stability was ultimately achieved when the Yawkey Trust hired John Harrington, who had worked as an accountant for Tom Yawkey in the 1970s. Harrington left the organization for a period to work in government and in the private sector before returning to the Sox.

In 1992, upon the death of Jean Yawkey, Harrington, acting as trustee for the Yawkey estate, bought out Sullivan's ownership share, eliminating the last managing general partner. Now, the Yawkey trust served as the majority owner of the franchise, free to run the Sox as it saw fit.

Jean Yawkey continued to seek the championship that had eluded her husband, though she was careful not to meddle in the day-to-day affairs of the team. Former GM Lou Gorman recalled that, on occasion, Yawkey would occasionally pop her head into Gorman's office at the end of off-season workdays, asking with hope in her voice, "Did we sign anyone today?"

Under Harrington's leadership, the Red Sox became one of the first pro sports franchises to develop and operate its own regional sports network (RSN), NESN, which continues to this day and is said to be the most profitable arm of the team's operations.

Also on his watch, the team moved its spring training headquarters from Winter Haven, Florida, to Fort Myers and attracted the 1999 All-Star Game, which included a stirring, memorable tribute to Ted Williams. Harrington himself became a major power broker among MLB owners, taking a leading role in labor negotiations during the 1994–95 strike and credited with advancing the concepts of divisional realignment and the introduction of the wild-card system.

On the field, the team won division titles in 1986, 1988, 1990, and 1995, and came within a strike of securing its first title in nearly 70 years before losing the 1986 World Series to the New York Mets.

In some ways, there exists a tangible connection to the team's past, and that includes the ties to Yawkey. That's logical enough, given that the club was owned by Yawkey himself, his widow, or his family's trust for nearly 70 years.

But in 2018, the current ownership group, headed by principal owner John Henry, officially changed the name of the street on which Fenway sits from Yawkey Way back to its original moniker of Jersey Street. (The street was renamed in honor of Yawkey a year after his passing.)

The reason, Henry made clear, was the team's troubled racial history—the stories of African American players being heckled off the field by a team official, and, of course, the fact that the Red Sox were the last MLB team to employ a Black player.

"I'm still haunted by what went on here a long time before we arrived," said Henry of the bid to return the street to its original name.

The move came at a time when politicians and other public officials were reviewing the propriety of honoring past figures whose words and actions, though perhaps indicative of their era, did not reflect current attitudes about race and civil rights.

The removal of statues of Confederate generals and soldiers was part of this reappraisal.

But in Boston, with its own complex racial history, the most obvious battleground happened around the local ballpark. Public hearings were held by the Boston Public Improvement Commission. City residents testified and so, too, did representatives of the Yawkey Foundation.

Some welcomed the change and expungement of Yawkey's name, however symbolic the gesture may have been. They believed it was appropriate to distance the team from its longtime owner.

Others complained that this was little more than the manifestation of political correctness, the very embodiment of revisionist virtue signaling.

In the end, controversy aside, the name change was largely symbolic. No signage will erase Yawkey's long ties to the franchise. He remains enshrined in Cooperstown, New York, home to the National Baseball Hall of Fame and Museum, an honor that rankles his many detractors.

But history is history, and while it can be viewed and interpreted differently with the passage of time, it cannot—nor should not—be erased.

Thomas A. Yawkey's imprint on the Red Sox franchise is forever. That includes his commitment to philanthropy; his love of the game; and his paternal attitude toward his players, as much as his unwillingness to integrate; his longtime employment of team officials who were known bigots; and, yes, his team's inability to win championships, which, in hindsight, may well have been at least partly a result of the absence of players of color for so long.

How different would Red Sox history have been had the team been more aggressive in signing Black players who followed in Robinson's footsteps and dominated National League baseball in the 1950s and 1960s: Willie Mays, Hank Aaron, Willie McCovey, Frank Robinson, Joe Morgan, Bob Gibson, Ernie Banks, Billy Williams, Maury Wills, Ferguson Jenkins, Roy Campanella, and Don Newcombe among them.

And just as it is impossible—and ill-advised—to separate the man from the team he owned, it's also inconceivable to draw a distinction between the man and his legacy.

He, like it, is complicated—perhaps highly so.

LOCALS

For any aspiring ballplayer, reaching the big leagues represents a dream come true. There can be no greater payoff for those who spend years perfecting the craft at the amateur level, then endure the long climb necessary to matriculate through the minor leagues.

Unless, of course, that journey culminates in doing so for the hometown team.

In the team's history, a number of Red Sox players have experienced the double thrill of getting to pro baseball's pinnacle and doing so in the uniform of the team for whom they grew up rooting.

If you grow up with an aim to reach the big leagues, the path is more challenging for those who grow up in New England. Unlike players who live in sunnier climes, New Englanders have much shorter seasons and often play spring games in winter-like conditions. They must also buck any biases on the part of scouts, who might tend to favor players in Florida, Texas, or California, where the players can be observed for a longer period, often against better competition.

Those who emerge from New England sandlots, however, often do so with a determination and mental toughness that others lack. If you can overcome cold, inclement weather, and facilities that aren't always first-rate, it might help—rather than hinder—your journey to the major leagues.

Over the decades, the Red Sox have had a number of All-Stars who learned the game in New England.

The best of these is probably Carlton Fisk, who was born in Vermont, but grew up across the Connecticut River—and state line—in Charlestown, New Hampshire. A first-round pick by the Red Sox in 1967, Fisk went on to play 10 seasons for the Sox, establishing himself as the best catcher in franchise history.

Fisk was a seven-time All-Star with the Sox and a unanimous choice for American League Rookie of the Year in 1972. Along the way, he earned his reputation as one of the team's top leaders, with a willingness to scrap. Fisk was a sturdy roadblock protecting the plate, despite a collision in 1974 that threatened to put an end to his career almost before it started. In subsequent collisions with Lou Piniella and rival Thurman Munson, both Yankees, Fisk helped initiate brawls that resulted in benches and bullpens emptying.

He hit one of the most famous home runs in World Series history in 1975, but the team's inability to tender him a contract on time in 1980 resulted in him being declared a free agent. Fisk would spend the final 13 years of his career with the White Sox, and a generation of fans never forgave Red Sox management for the contractual screwup.

When Fisk retired, he was 45 years old and held major league marks for most career homers by a catcher as well as games played. He was elected to the Hall of Fame and chose to be represented by his Red Sox cap, undoubtedly further triggering Red Sox fans who could only imagine what was lost by not having Fisk spend his entire career in Boston.

At least Fisk's career had a happy ending, which could not be said of Tony Conigliaro.

A native of the North Shore of Massachusetts—born in Revere, raised in Swampscott, and schooled in Lynn—Conigliaro was a schoolboy star who signed with the Sox as a 17-year-old and was in the big leagues less than two years later, having never played above Single A in the minors.

Throughout his career, Conigliaro would show a flair for the dramatic, and that penchant began on Opening Day of the 1964 season, when Conigliaro homered at Fenway in his first major league at-bat. The following year, he became baseball's youngest home-run champion, leading the American League with 32 homers at 20 years of age.

In 1967, he was chosen as an All-Star and headed for his best season yet when, on a Friday night in

August, Conigliaro was struck in the face by a pitch from California's Jack Hamilton. The sound of the impact resulted in a sickening thud as the ball rolled across the infield grass. Conigliaro was rushed to the hospital. He suffered a broken cheekbone, a dislocated jaw, and a badly damaged left retina.

Only weeks earlier, he had become the youngest player in history to reach 100 homers for his career. Now, it was doubtful he would play again.

Incredibly, however, Conigliaro returned to the Red Sox in 1969, and true to form, hit a game-winning, extra-inning home run in his first game back. Conigliaro won Comeback Player of the Year and a year later, posted career highs in both homers (36) and RBI (116). But the Red Sox, sensing that Conigliaro's vision was deteriorating, traded him to the California Angels. After a year with the Angels, Conigliaro indeed retired at the age of 26.

Following a three-year layoff, Conigliaro toyed with the idea of a comeback—this time as a pitcher. Eventually, he returned as a DH and made the Red Sox out of spring training, but a month into the season, he retired for good. No less an authority than Hall of Fame pitcher Jim Palmer has stated that he believed Conigliaro had the ability to become baseball's all-time home run king.

Movie-star handsome, Conigliaro tried his hand at sportscasting for two years after his playing career ended, but in 1982, he suffered a heart attack, and later a stroke, resulting in brain damage. He died eight years later at 45.

Conigliaro's career was filled with promise but sadly brief. Still, the lessons learned from his perseverance remain to this day.

There must be something about the catching position and New England natives who went on to play for the Sox. Fisk remains the gold standard, but he's hardly alone.

Rich Gedman, born in Worcester, starred for the Sox in the 1980s. Gedman was undrafted out of high school but signed with the Sox as a free agent and agreed to try catching. Three years later, he made his major league debut, pinch-hitting for, of all people, Carl Yastrzemski.

In 1981, his first full season with the team, he essentially replaced Fisk as the team's starting catcher. In 11 seasons, he was a two-time All-Star, a Rookie of the Year runner-up, a member of the 1986 pennant-winning club, and the batterymate in Roger Clemens' first 20-strikeout performance.

Two other New Englanders—Mike Ryan of Haverhill, Massachusetts, and Russ Gibson of Fall River—were the catching tandem for the Sox during the 1967 Impossible Dream season.

A decade earlier, Malden, Massachusetts, native Bill Monbouquette began an 11-year pitching career in the big leagues, the first eight of which were spent with the Sox. For some moribund Red Sox teams of the early 1960s, Monbouquette was sometimes the only starting pitcher of note, winning in double figures every year from 1960 through 1965, including a 20-win season in 1963.

Over a 13-year MLB career, Walt Dropo of Moosup, Connecticut, won Rookie of the Year honors while with the Sox in 1950, but was traded just two years later, and spent 10 more seasons in the majors, never to achieve the success he had in his first full big-league season.

There are, of course, many others—including Jerry Remy, profiled elsewhere in this book—who played anywhere from several games to several seasons for the Red Sox. Each has his own story to tell, some longer than others.

None, though, ever forgot his first opportunity—whether it lasted for a homestand or a career—to represent the local team.

3

The Henry Era

For a team whose origin story dates to 1901, it's remarkable to consider that the Red Sox have been helmed by two ownership groups since 1933.

From 1933 to 1976, the team was owned by Thomas A. Yawkey. From 1976 until Jean Yawkey passed in 1992, ownership was controlled by a group led by his widow, after which the club was owned by the Yawkey Trust for a decade before being sold to a group led by John Henry.

One team, nearly 90 years, and just two owners.

It's not at all hyperbolic to say that Henry's arrival ushered in the greatest era in franchise history, with four championships won in the first 20 years of his tenure—to say nothing of a complete rehabilitation of a ballpark that had long ago seen its best days.

What's remarkable is the skepticism and outright hostility that greeted his arrival.

When the Yawkey estate, under the direction of managing general partner John Harrington, having failed in its efforts to get a replacement built for Fenway, put the team up for sale in 2001, the overriding wish of most fans was for local ownership.

Yawkey wasn't a Boston native, having been born in Michigan with roots in South Carolina. But as much as a non-native can, Yawkey, though his commitment to the franchise and to several charities, became an honorary New Englander and never wavered in his dedication to keeping the Red Sox in Boston (though he briefly flirted with thoughts of a shift to the suburbs in the mid-1960s).

In the years before the Sox were up for auction, the fate of the New England Patriots was very much in doubt. For a time, they were in danger of being moved to St. Louis. When Robert Kraft purchased them in 1994, he nearly moved them to Hartford, where, technically, they would have remained the New England Patriots, but most assuredly not of Massachusetts.

Eventually, Kraft abandoned the idea of going to Connecticut and privately funded the construction of a new stadium to keep the team in Foxboro. But the specter of seeing their football team nearly whisked out of state had shaken the region's sports fans. The last thing they wanted was an ownership group without roots in the region.

Like it not, however, that's what they soon got. While Boston concessionaire and philanthropist Joe O'Donnell mounted a bid and became the unofficial choice of most Sox fans to purchase the team, Major League Baseball and developer Frank McCourt proposed a replacement Fenway on the Boston waterfront. Commissioner Bud Selig had other ideas.

Selig was instrumental in arranging a shotgun marriage involving Henry, Werner, and Larry Lucchino. The three had no real connections to Boston—or, for that matter, in some instances, one another.

Henry had bought the Florida Marlins in 1999 after earlier owning a minor stake in the Yankees, the latter of which alone would have been enough for many Red Sox fans to disqualify him from owning the Red Sox.

Werner, meanwhile, had been part-owner of the San Diego Padres, during which time the most noteworthy thing about the franchise was comedian Roseanne Barr's ill-fated attempt at humor when singing the National Anthem. Barr, in a poorly conceived bit of satire, decided it would be a good idea to grab her crotch and spit, a commentary on the slovenly habits of the modern ballplayer.

The stunt backfired in a big way, and Werner, who had been a producer of Barr's popular TV show, was tried and convicted in the court of public opinion.

Lucchino, meanwhile, lacked the financial wherewithal to own a team, but had been president of both the Baltimore Orioles—as a mentee of famed litigator Edward Bennett Williams—and later, the Padres.

Werner and Lucchino were already aligned, but together lacked the deep pockets necessary to first win the bidding, then operate the team as the big-market behemoth it was. Enter Henry, who, in addition to owning the Marlins, had toyed with buying the Angels and had briefly been in pursuit of for both NBA and NHL franchises.

If Lucchino brought the gravitas and legal expertise and Werner an understanding of media, Henry brought the big bucks. United, they became greater than the sum of their parts.

But Selig saw promise in this trio. Part of that belief may have been steeped in expediency—with Henry and Werner already having been vetted as owners and Lucchino a respected figure around the game, Selig knew that, at the very least, the three would not have difficulty getting approval from their fellow owners.

Selig effectively placed his thumb on the scale and steered the sale toward Henry and Co. Their bid of $640 million, plus another $60 million assumption of debt, entitled the group to the franchise, Fenway Park, and 80 percent ownership in the New England Sports Network (NESN), a regional sports TV network that broadcast the team's games and those of its partners, the NHL's Boston Bruins.

Once the winning bid was accepted by the Yawkey estate, approval from ownership was seen as a *fait accompli.* When the vote came through, Lucchino opened a window from a suite in the team's spring training headquarters and extended his arm with a thumbs-up, while inside, champagne popped from bottles and flowed.

From the beginning, realizing that it needed to win over wary Red Sox fans who feared an infestation of carpetbaggers, Henry and Co. pledged their commitment and loyalty to the team and the city.

Alone among the bidders, the Henry group promised fealty to Fenway. (At the time, the dedication to Fenway was publicly portrayed as a sign of the owners' recognition of the importance of tradition; in truth, it was equally motivated by economics. The city of Boston and the commonwealth, through its refusal to shoulder the cost of replacing both Sullivan Stadium in Foxboro and the Boston Garden, longtime home of the Bruins and Celtics, had already demonstrated that public funds would not be spent on new pro sports facilities, and having spent more than two-thirds of a billion dollars to execute the purchase, Henry, Werner, and Lucchino had neither the stomach nor the funding to construct Fenway II.)

It didn't take long for the new owners to make their mark. Within days of being approved, they jettisoned GM Dan Duquette as well as manager Joe Kerrigan, whose appointment the previous summer as a replacement for Jimy Williams had proved disastrous.

In their place, the Sox installed veteran MLB executive Mike Port as an interim GM, while hiring Grady Little as manager. The latter choice was so instantly popular with the players that they could be heard cheering wildly when their new manager was introduced in the middle of a closed-door clubhouse meeting.

With that, they were off and running.

In some ways, Henry was the right person at the right time to purchase the Sox. At the exact time the game was giving way to the analytics revolution and reassessing how it measured the performance of players, Henry came from a background in mathematics and quantitative analysis.

Working in hedge funds, it was Henry's job to evaluate risk and reward, which he did with great success. He also had a passion for the game. Growing up—first in Illinois and later in Arkansas—Henry was the son of a farmer. When his father died when he was just 26, Henry, having studied the commodities market, purchased then sold off his shares for great profit.

His interest in predicting futures markets and selling assets at precisely the right time would soon result in Henry developing his own formula for investing and establishing his own investment company.

But Henry had a passion for baseball. Born a Cardinals fan who listened to games on the radio and revered Hall of Famer Stan Musial, Henry played APBA Baseball—a rudimentary simulation game—as a boy and was later an early fan of fantasy baseball. Even as he built a financial empire, Henry encouraged his employees to compete against him.

* * *

It didn't take long for Henry to become involved in the day-to-day goings-on of his baseball team. After hiring next-gen baseball executive Billy Beane as his GM, only to have Beane back out of the deal within hours, he trusted his instincts and promoted from within, elevating assistant GM Theo Epstein to become, at 28, the youngest GM in the game's history.

In 2003, in a bit of foreshadowing, Henry began to worry about the suitability of Little as his manager. Too often, Henry believed, Little was making moves based on instinct rather than statistical evidence.

That summer, he summoned those who followed the team daily—beat writers, TV and radio announcers, and analysts—and asked them the same question: "Do I have the right manager for this team?"

That fall, the Red Sox qualified for the postseason for the first time since Henry and Co. took over, but his uncertainty over Little's suitability proved prescient. In the deciding Game 7 of the American League Championship Series in Yankee Stadium, Little opted to stay with ace Pedro Martinez when the pitcher was clearly tiring and ineffective.

On one hand, Little's decision-making process was understandable. The Red Sox's bullpen had been problematic most of the season, and in the moment, the manager opted to take his chances with arguably the greatest pitcher in franchise history. But in so doing, he also ignored the evidence, which revealed—as it would for most pitchers—that Martinez became far less effective as his pitch count climbed north of 90.

Sure enough, the Yankees rallied to tie the game off Martinez in the eighth, and in the 11th, starter-cum-reliever Tim Wakefield surrendered a game-winning, series-clinching, season-ending home run. Even by Red Sox historic standards, this was a crushing blow.

Little was fired within days. Henry was determined to find the right man as a replacement but allowed Epstein and Lucchino to conduct the search.

"More than anything else," Henry told ESPN, "management is a question of ensuring you have the right people in place and they have the resources necessary to be successful."

What followed, after the hiring of Terry Francona, was the most successful 15-year-long stretch in franchise history, culminating in four championships—nearly equal to the number of titles won by the team in the previous century.

Henry authorized payrolls that were among the largest in the game—in the first 20 years, they were among the top five spenders in Major League Baseball every year but three and often were ranked either first or second.

He's been unafraid of challenging orthodoxy. Soon after taking over, he hired pioneering analytics guru Bill James, who offered his input on what personnel moves the club should consider, using his own predictive models. Such a move may now be commonplace through the game, with teams building entire staffs devoted to data analysis, but at the time, it was both groundbreaking and hotly debated.

For the most part, Henry stood loyal to his operating principles by remaining out of the way, while occasionally providing advice, or sometimes, simple encouragement. Francona revealed that he often received emails when things weren't going well with middle-of-the-night timestamps, an indication to the manager that the owner, too, was having trouble sleeping after a particularly frustrating loss.

But occasionally Henry strayed from his own advice and injected himself. Alarmed by the team's precipitous drop out of wild-card contention in the final month of the 2011 season, he determined that Francona, following two World Series rings, another trip to the ALCS, and five postseason trips in eight tries, had run his course in Boston and refused to pick up a team option.

Epstein himself wondered if it was time for a new challenge and, though under contract, negotiated his way free to become president of baseball operations for the Chicago Cubs.

After nine seasons of Henry's ownership, the Red Sox were at a crossroads. Lucchino overruled new GM Ben Cherington and chose Bobby Valentine to replace Francona in the dugout. The pick couldn't have been more calamitous. Valentine, who hadn't managed in the big leagues for the past decade, proved to be hopelessly inept, alienating players and coaches alike while overseeing a last-place finish.

The 2013 season saw the Sox with their third manager (former Sox pitching coach John Farrell) in as many seasons and a return to glory with last-place-to-first turnaround and a most unforeseen championship.

Along the way, Henry's sports holdings grew. Fenway Sports Group, the parent company that oversees the Sox, also purchased Liverpool F.C. of the Premier League, along with Roush (NASCAR) Racing and the NHL's Pittsburgh Penguins.

Those additional investments helped foster some concern among Red Sox fans that Henry wasn't as dedicated to the on-field success of the team and saw it only as a cash cow through which he could expand his business empire. That proved unfounded.

In an effort to change the team's sullied reputation on the matter of inclusiveness, the Sox have made significant strides. Under Henry, the organization hired its first manager of color (Alex Cora); promoted Raquel Ferreira to a senior position, making her one of the highest-ranking women in the industry; and achieved other firsts, including the hiring of the first female coach of color as a minor league instructor.

To some, those moves might be written off as "virtue signaling" or mere political correctness. But given the team's history in that area, they can't help but be viewed as meaningful steps of progress, as the Red Sox move purposefully from their own past.

Still, the team's up-and-down performance in the second decade of the 21st century—two World Series, but also, four last-place finishes between 2012 and 2020—served to drive Henry underground when it came to visibility.

Never comfortable in the spotlight, he bristled at suggestions of instability—though four managers and three lead baseball executives in the span of eight seasons suggested there was something to the charge—and once bizarrely maintained that the club had become too enthralled with analytics, at a time when the entire sport was clearly moving in the direction that his own club had once pioneered.

Soft-spoken and reserved by nature, Henry became far less accessible to the media, turning back interview requests. Invariably, he would become frustrated with himself in his press availabilities for having said something he believed to be relatively benign, only to see it become a flashpoint for controversy.

(A 2011 radio interview with 98.5 The Sports Hub, one of two sports talk stations in Boston, proved ill-advised to say the least. Frustrated with criticism of how the Sox were being operated, Henry drove himself to the radio station and, unannounced, invited himself into the studio for a freewheeling and contentious interview. It was hardly his finest hour, and the interview lives on in infamy.)

Henry's purchase of the *Boston Globe* in 2013 proved controversial as well. Under Henry, the Globe's editorial page remains one of liberal advocacy, an ideological stance that puts him at odds with segments of the team's fan base. Some have charged, without evidence or merit, that he has quashed any critical dissent, or that Henry seized control of New England's largest daily newspaper to ensure only favorable coverage of his baseball team. In truth, neither allegation is accurate.

* * *

Beyond the team's accomplishments on the field, the Henry ownership group oversaw monumental changes.

It completed a renovation of Fenway Park that transpired over a 12-year stretch. In most obvious ways, the ballpark is still the same: the Green Monster is still, better than a century after the park's construction, its most identifiable aspect. Whether you're viewing it in person or on a telecast, it's the single most recognizable part of the facility.

Other elements remain unchanged, too: the bleachers, some inexplicably situated at a strange angle, forcing fans to crane their necks to focus on the action on the field. The lack of nearby parking and cramped wooden grandstand seats remain, too.

But in other ways, Fenway is barely recognizable. The Monster Seats proved to be a fan favorite, and the installation of new video scoreboards throughout the ballpark, along with additional points of sale for concessions and wider concourses, have served to modernize the ballpark. The Sox have also sought to maximize the seating capacity, increasing to the point where the ballpark's capacity is about 2,000 seats more than when it was last sold.

The Red Sox have also expertly maximized use of the ballpark for marketing through signage and other merchandising. Some have been put off by such signs of overt commercialism, but Henry makes no apologies.

"You can't win in any sport without heavily concentrating on revenue generation," he told ESPN. "You have to be relentless in that regard if you are going to afford the kind of players you need to compete at the highest level."

In keeping with that philosophy, ticket prices for Red Sox games remain among the highest in the game.

But where once the ballpark seemed hopelessly obsolete, its 21st century makeover has resulted in it becoming a cash cow, as much a tourist attraction—tour groups cycle through the ballpark year-round—as other Boston landmarks.

Henry's legacy ultimately remains on display in the team's trophy case, where evidence of four World Series triumphs sits. If he's not always the most effective communicator or a willing face of the franchise he owns, Henry has made good on his original promise to treat the Red Sox as a "public trust." And there can be no arguing with the success the team has enjoyed on his watch.

PART 2

THE MEDIA

4

Ned Martin

Ned Martin's time behind the microphone, describing Red Sox action on TV and radio, spanned a generation, from 1961 to 1992.

In that time, nearly everything about the game changed, often dramatically. When Martin began, the Red Sox were part of a 10-team American League. There were no playoffs, just the ultimate payoff each October.

The Red Sox's roster had been integrated only two years prior to his arrival. He had missed calling games involving Ted Williams by a mere season. Doubleheaders were prevalent, only a portion of the schedule was televised, and radio and newspapers were the daily conduits through which fans stayed connected to a team.

By the time Martin retired in 1992, Major League Baseball had grown from 20 to 28 teams, the leagues had divided into two divisions, and shortly, expansion would bring two more teams and a three-division alignment.

Fenway went from an often sparsely attended relic to a charming traditional ballpark, the model for a new generation of ballparks that was just beginning. As a franchise, the Red Sox went from cellar-dwelling and often irrelevant, headlined by a single star or two, to a far more consistent bunch, in contention more often than out, even if their decades-long quest for a title wasn't completed until two years after Martin's passing in 2002.

Martin witnessed the arrival of the DH, baseball's westward expansion, the proliferation of artificial turf and garish polyester uniforms. He was part of baseball's initial foray into cable TV, even as he maintained a sentimental preference for radio.

His first broadcast dovetailed with the arrival of the new left fielder, Carl Yastrzemski, and his career spanned the entirety of Yaz's career—plus an additional 10 seasons.

He was there through it all, traversing the expanse, surviving the changes, a constant to a generation of Red Sox fans who regarded him as their constant companion, relaying the events of West Coast games past midnight back to New England.

His was the voice emanating from the transistor on a beach blanket on the Cape or a weekend cookout on the North Shore, or providing reassuring, familiar company for a long drive on a summer's night.

When Martin interrupted his game description to remind listeners "to have a Gansett"—Narragansett Beer was a longtime broadcast sponsor—he could have been an inviting neighbor, leaning over a backyard fence.

But Martin was so much more than a broadcaster, or, as they were commonly known when his career began, an "announcer." Though he described growing up in the suburbs northwest of

Philadelphia as more rural than might be expected, attending "an old country schoolhouse," Martin was far from some rube.

To the contrary, he attended Duke University and, as a young man, developed a fondness for the English language. He was learned in Shakespeare's sonnets and Hemingway's novels and could quote either effortlessly without the least bit of artifice or pretense.

He would pass time on the road visiting museums or historic sites, delighting in the opportunity to learn and enrich and educate himself.

Like Vin Scully, situated thousands of miles away on the West Coast, and a few other contemporaries, Martin was less a play-by-plan man and more of an expert storyteller. To hold a listener's attention—and perhaps to guard against his own boredom—Martin peppered his calls with references to literature and history.

It was only fitting, in retrospect, that the baseball team that had been celebrated by literary icons like John Updike and noted scholars like Doris Kearns Goodwin would have as one of its broadcast voices a man who appreciated literature, history, and the power of the English language.

In Martin, the Red Sox had all that and more.

Martin's erudition was never mistaken for pomposity. The literary references didn't clutter the broadcast; they merely added to it, offering another portal through which fans could enjoy the game.

But Martin's deep love of the English language didn't always manifest itself with allusions that might have gone over the head of most. It was the way he incorporated his vocabulary into his game descriptions, often searching for—and finding—the perfect word, the most apt verb.

"It isn't an awful thing to have a vocabulary and use it," Martin, more than a bit defensively, once told the *Boston Globe.*

Indeed, it was not. So, Martin injected his calls with colorful phrasing. Balls didn't just bounce off Fenway's Green Monster—they "caromed." Leads weren't merely slight—they were "tenuous."

Occasionally, Martin, for all his education and command of the language, found that a simple exclamation could convey his amazement at what had just transpired on the field. Perhaps it was a particularly acrobatic catch in the outfield or a blazing exhibition of speed on the basepaths that left Martin at somewhat of a loss.

"Mercy," he would utter, and listeners innately understood that something remarkable had taken place. Martin's style was decidedly understated; he allowed games to breathe, to assume their natural pace. He also had the benefit of not having to cram in countless "drop-ins"—quick ads interspersed into the action that can upend the rhythm of a broadcast and which now serve as the bane of many current-day broadcasters, forced to disrupt the natural flow in service to sponsors. Some of that skill was learned on radio, where the medium allows for an unhurried tempo.

(Ironically, when Martin was dropped by a new flagship radio station in 1979, it was said to be partly motivated by the fact that he had treated the growing number of drop-ins with audible disdain.)

That sort of boyish wonderment served Martin particularly well during the magical 1967 Impossible Dream season. Once, after the team that had earned the sobriquet "Cardiac Kids" for its habit of staging improbable come-from-behind wins staged yet another improbable comeback, Martin issued this on-air reset: "If you've just turned your radio on, it's happened again."

And fittingly, it was Martin who was on the TV call when the Red Sox clinched the 1967 pennant with a win in the final game of the season over the Minnesota Twins. The Sox had somehow emerged from a thicket of contenders on the final weekend. As Minnesota's Rich Rollins made the final out on a soft, arching liner to shallow left, Martin's genius for calling the action was on display as the Red Sox qualified for the World Series for the first time in more than two decades.

"Looped toward shortstop...[Rico] Petrocelli's back...he's got it! The Red Sox win.... And there's pandemonium on the field.... Listen!"

The latter instruction would be unimaginable today, where a more self-conscious broadcaster might instead be ready to read from a prepared monologue.

Martin would have none of that. He knew that no matter his eloquence, the best soundtrack to this historic moment in franchise history would be the elation felt by the fans who had stormed the field, surrounding the players and becoming part of the celebration itself.

He was also at the microphone for so many signature events and milestones—the 1975 World Series and Carlton Fisk's historic, game-winning homer in Game 6, which he broadcast on national radio; Yastrzemski's 400th homer and 3,000th career base hit; and Yaz's final regular season game in 1983. Given that Martin broke in as a Red Sox announcer when Yastrzemski was in his rookie season, that one had to have special significance.

But Martin's real charm wasn't always typified by the Big Moment, or the games of greatest consequence. Often, it was most evident in the humdrum, one more game in a long season. It could be a quip or a particularly artful turn of phrase that could enliven a lopsided loss or further enhance a runaway victory.

"Red Smith used to say he loved 'the music of the game.' What a great line," Martin once told author Curt Smith. "There is a lot of music to it, whether it's the first crack of the bat at Winter Haven, a full house on Opening Day, the murmuration of a meaningless game in July or the buzz you feel at a World Series.

"You can still see something in almost every game that you've never seen before. That's the beauty of baseball, I guess."

Well, that, and having the privilege of listening to a firsthand account of a game by someone like Martin.

Martin was your daily companion on a twisting, six-month-long journey and his mere presence was reassuring.

He teamed with a long list of partners. Some were fellow broadcast professionals, like Ken Coleman, whose Red Sox broadcasting career, even interrupted by stints in Cleveland, was also long and meritorious; some were ex-Red Sox players, like Johnny Pesky or Mel Parnell.

But one partner in particular proved to be Martin's broadcasting soulmate. Jim Woods, who had been the No. 2 announcer in other stops with Jack Buck, Mel Allen, and Red Barber, fit Martin's style perfectly. Woods was something of a raconteur and his folksy style perfectly complemented Martin's more cerebral approach.

Martin would come to affectionately call Woods "Possum," and the two formed one of the most beloved baseball broadcast teams of all time. *Baseball Magazine* named them the best duo of the 1970s.

Though their audience were, by definition, Red Sox fans, Martin and Woods weren't about to deceive their listeners about what was taking place on the field. If a poor play was committed, or a lack of hustle was evident by the home team, Martin and Woods weren't afraid to recognize it.

But they left little doubt as to their true rooting interests. Once, when Kansas City Royals manager Whitey Herzog walked a Red Sox hitter intentionally to pitch instead to Carl Yastrzemski, the move backfired in a big way when Yaz delivered a go-ahead hit.

As Yastrzemski rounded first and the run crossed the plate, Woods couldn't contain his glee.

"There goes your strategy, Mr. Herzog!" exclaimed Woods, taking equal delight at the manager's misstep and Yaz's heroics.

Sadly, the 1978 one-game playoff defeat to the New York Yankees marked Martin's final game as the team's radio voice. He and Woods were not renewed, with the station owner noting that it wanted announcers who were more comfortable schmoozing advertising clients before and after games.

Thankfully, Martin's career as a Red Sox voice was far from over. For the next 14 years, he worked as the lead play-by-play man on, first, Channel 38 (WSBK-TV) and later, New England Sports Network (NESN), the regional sports network in which the Red Sox themselves had an 80 percent ownership stake.

Martin's style may have been better suited for radio, but he adapted well enough to the demands of the television medium. Paired with a succession of former players—from Ken Harrelson to former backup catcher Bob Montgomery to, finally, Jerry Remy—Martin's breezy style adapted to the medium.

When Channel 38 moved on from him, saying that he lacked pizzazz, Martin, self-effacing and aware of his own strengths and weaknesses, didn't put up much of an argument: "Pizzazz? No, I'm afraid that just isn't me."

That was no indictment, of course. Martin was far less interested in generating artificial excitement or changing his natural persona to fit TV's demands. His charge, as he saw it, was to inform and entertain, and do so in his own natural manner.

In 2000, Martin, out of the booth for nearly a decade by then, was inducted into the Red Sox Hall of Fame. A standing ovation from those in attendance at the event appeared to surprise Martin, who, privately, had wondered if he had been forgotten since his retirement. The warm welcome told him otherwise.

"Until then," Joe Castiglione, the longtime Red Sox radio voice, told Smith, "I don't think he knew how much he was loved. He was a most modest guy."

After his passing in 2002, Martin was posthumously inducted into the Massachusetts Broadcasters Hall of Fame, though oddly, he was never recognized with the one award due him: the Ford Frick Award, given annually for "commitment to excellence, quality of broadcasting abilities, reverence within the game, popularity with fans, and recognition by peers."

Martin met all those qualifiers without a doubt but was never given the honor. Surely, that reflects more on the voters than Martin himself. It's possible that Martin was denied the award because of the very thing that endeared to him to so many: his disdain for self-promotion.

But a list of baseball's best broadcasters that doesn't include Edwin "Ned" Martin III?

Mercy.

5

Peter Gammons

By the late 1960s, baseball coverage in daily newspapers had become more than a little anachronistic. (In the decades to come, newspapers themselves would follow suit. But I digress.)

Before the arrival of the internet, before the proliferation of cable, before the explosion of talk radio, newspapers were the main conduit to the sports world.

In that era, newspaper reporters were like characters out of *The Front Page*—Damon Runyonesque, right down to the cigar-chomping, hard-drinking stereotypes from a bygone era.

At the time, reporters often traveled with the team, with some doing so at the team's expense. Incredibly, few seemed troubled by this blatant conflict of interest.

With few exceptions, these reporters were locked in a bygone era. They wrote in flowery language more fitting for World War II. Lefthanded pitchers were "southpaws." Infielders were "second sackers," or perhaps they patrolled "the hot corner."

Many—either because of their indebtedness to the teams they covered, or out of willful ignorance—were apologists for management. The burgeoning Players Association, which began in the mid- to late 1960s, was seen as a radical movement, bent on destroying the national pastime. Players who held out in salary disputes were seen as misguided at best, greedy at worst.

The introduction of a labor union representing the players was an affront to the game. The existence of the reserve clause, which effectively bound players to their original teams either for life or until the team no longer benefited from them, was shrugged off.

For the most part, reporters didn't rock the boat. Many wrote what they were told by management or ownership and didn't question being utilized as unpaid flacks for the teams they were ostensibly covering.

Until the 1950s, when, among others, Dick Young in New York began the practice of interviewing players in the clubhouse postgame, many reporters wrote only what they saw between the first and ninth innings. Off-field disputes between manager and player over playing time or between player and management over salary were glossed over.

The game was the thing, and most game accounts read like dry toast, with little flavor, and certainly no opinion: *Carl Yastrzemski homered and knocked in three runs and Dave Morehead pitched seven innings of four-hit ball as the Boston Red Sox beat the Detroit Tigers 5–1 before a crowd of 17,426 at Fenway Park Monday...*

Such was the baseball beat: rat-a-tat writing style, outmoded language, and a see-no-evil approach to anything with a hint of controversy.

Into this staid, conventional world in the late 1960s came Peter Gammons, son of Groton, Massachusetts, recent graduate of the University of North Carolina, and debtor to no one.

Gammons began his career at the *Boston Globe* the same week as a recent graduate of Boston College, Bob Ryan, and together, the two shared their first *Globe* byline: a new story on the decision by professional sports leagues to play games as scheduled in the aftermath of the assassination of Sen. Robert F. Kennedy.

After a period during which he served as a general assignment reporter in the sports department, Gammons was placed on the Red Sox beat. It's not hyperbolic to suggest that the business of covering a Major League Baseball beat would never be the same again.

Gammons didn't set out to revolutionize the industry. That was neither his ambition nor his personality.

But at 24, he brought an undeniably different and fresh perspective to the job. He wasn't beholden to tradition, nor meek enough to conform simply because "that's the way it's always been done."

It helped that his bosses at the *Globe* allowed—encouraged, in some cases—a more youthful and slightly more irreverent approach.

For one thing, Gammons was scarcely older than most of the players, and, in fact, not as old as some. This provided him with an immediate connection. Like some of the players he was covering, he wore his hair longer, dressed more casually and colorfully, and listened to rock 'n' roll.

All these things provided an opening to relate more easily to many players on the roster. If Gammons, son of a minister, hardly qualified as a wide-eyed radical, neither was he old enough to be the father (or grandfather) of the players, part of the establishment.

Gammons quickly established relationships. Youthful and with no shortage of energy—decades later, Gammons' vitality, with his habit of sleeping only three or four hours nightly, would shock those half his age—he quickly blended in with much of the roster.

It was not unusual, at a time when access was granted more casually and without nearly the restrictions that exist today, for him to show up hours ahead of the rest of the beat and shag fly balls in the outfield during early batting practice.

Whereas his forebears had played card games and drunk with management, Gammons quickly bonded with the players, who were more his contemporaries.

But while Gammons had the vigor to work up a daily sweat alongside the players, what set him apart from his more seasoned colleagues was his effort to forge relationships throughout the game. He began assembling a cadre of scouts, executives, and coaches from whom he could glean information.

Who was on the trading block? Which players were underachieving? What moves were being contemplated?

This type of intellectual curiosity was, surprisingly, rare for the industry. Too many of his predecessors were content to chronicle the hits, runs, and errors on the field while failing to seek out any of the intriguing back stories.

Two things soon proved revolutionary about the coverage Gammons provided *Globe* readers.

First, he introduced thorough accounting of the team's minor leagues through a weekly column called "Majoring in the Minors." At the time, there was no *Baseball America*, and, of course, no internet. Prospects playing in Louisville (the site of the organization's Triple A affiliate) or Pittsfield, Massachusetts, (where the Double A team was housed) might as well have been playing on the moon.

There were no updates on which young players were developing and which ones had stalled. By introducing regular coverage of the team's minor league system, Gammons connected his readers to the team's top prospects. Suddenly, these weren't just faceless prospects in far-flung outposts; they were real, living minor leaguers, some of them mere months from arriving at—and contributing to—the parent club.

But by far Gammons' biggest breakthrough was the development of his "Sunday Baseball Notes" column. This would prove not only revolutionary to coverage of the sport but also influential in the evolution of sports sections.

Until then, sports coverage tended to focus solely on the day-to-day goings-on. There were game stories, which relayed the who, what, when, and where of the previous night's game. Perhaps a few tidbits were tacked on at the end, updating the status of injured players or explaining a lineup change.

The information gathered for the Sunday notes was different. First, while the primary focus remained on the Red Sox, they weren't the lone reference point. Gammons accumulated tidbits throughout the week from his army of sources—scouts, coaches, rival players, managers, and executives across the game. Daily, Gammons would accumulate informative nuggets from his time near the batting cage during batting practice, but not all of it would fit snugly into his daily coverage of the Sox. He would hear of trade proposals, or plans to promote a hot prospect or reduce a struggling veteran's playing time. He'd be told which manager was on the hot seat, which replacements were being considered.

Scouts would offer their assessment of what they'd seen—who was hot and who was not. Why was a star player slumping and exactly who is that hot-shot rookie tearing up the league? Gammons was embedded in the game, and in short order, his legion of contacts trumped those of any competitor.

All of this was done, of course, prior to the invention of smartphones. In his day, he couldn't simply text a general manager or a scouting director. He either called them on the phone, or, through his regular coverage of the Red Sox, spoke to them person-to-person: on the field, in the ballpark dining room, in the hotel bar, or in the clubhouse.

His energy was boundless and his enthusiasm unmatched.

"His contacts, he had them everywhere," said longtime sportswriter Chaz Scoggins, who was on the Red Sox beat in the 1970s and 1980s when Gammons reigned. "He was a workaholic, completely tireless, and I'm sure he wrote five times more than what got in the *Globe*. He was constantly on the phone, constantly writing. His work ethic was incredible, on top of being a brilliant writer."

Gammons had never played the game at an elevated level, but his deep appreciation for it and his tireless work ethic helped earn him the respect of the people in the game. If Gammons was willing to put in the time to ask about the development of a new pitch, or an adjustment in a hitter's stance, they were, in turn, willing to share their process.

Gaining the trust of front office executives was different, because the stakes were higher. If a proposed trade were to leak prematurely, it could jeopardize its completion. But then, Gammons had gained the hard-earned trust of his coterie of sources—if they told him to hold on to the information for a bit, he would; if he were asked to withhold a detail or two, he'd do that, too.

Each Sunday, information-starved baseball fans would consume the Sunday Baseball Notes whole, delighting in the tidbits of information presented not just about the Red Sox, but their rivals as well. In no time, it became required reading—not just among fans, but those in the industry, too.

And, in keeping with the changes that were sweeping the game, Gammons' work didn't stop after the season. He was particularly insightful in the run-up to the annual Winter Meetings, the game's December gathering that brought GMs, agents, and scouts all under one roof, and where most off-season transactions were completed.

Leading up to the meetings, Gammons would outline which teams were eager to fill which roster needs. In their aftermath, he would relay a slew of trades that almost happened or might soon be revisited.

This comprehensive coverage soon became a staple of sports sections across the country. Imitation is the sincerest form of flattery, and sports editors felt the need to match the depth and breadth of the reporting offered by Gammons—in all sports. The fact that few—if any—had the contacts, tenacity, or institutional knowledge to which Gammons could lay claim was almost incidental. They at least had to make the effort.

Beyond the revolution he helped usher in in terms of his reporting and resources, there was also the matter of writing style.

Gammons wasn't bound by conventional newspaper style. His more freewheeling prose—peppered with references to hidden New England outposts or augmented by a song lyric—resonated with younger readers, who connected with him generationally.

As Tom Wolfe's New Journalism took hold, younger readers wanted—no, *expected*—more. They were less interested in how the runs were scored than they were in an explanation of why the Red Sox won or lost. Gammons delivered that insight as few others could, and he did so in a less conventional manner.

"He took it from just straight baseball reporting to literature, in my opinion," Scoggins said. "His ledes were just different than everybody else's. I marveled at them sometimes. His vocabulary was tremendous, his prose was incredible. It just flowed out of him like crazy. While everyone else was writing AP-style ledes, he would describe a home run like, 'It came up like the sun over Campobello Island.' I was just...who writes like that?"

Not everyone was enamored with his less-than-traditional game stories.

"I wish," groused a competitor once, "that I didn't have to get to the sixth graf to get the final score."

But that, too, was an example of Gammons being ahead of the curve.

Before too long, the existence of ESPN's *SportsCenter*—and countless imitators, chock-full of highlights—would force yet another change in newspaper coverage. It would make little sense to provide 12-hour-old accounts of games that had already been seen, the important parts of which were endlessly rerun and available hour after hour.

Gammons would also spend a stint at *Sports Illustrated*, but that was limiting. For a time, the magazine deadlines rendered some of his "notes columns" dated. And even his features didn't do him justice. After New England readers were accustomed to reading him on an almost daily basis, year-round, who wanted to be restricted to just one—maximum—Gammons story a week?

In time, Gammons would also be among the first generation of newspaper reporters to make the transition to TV, where their reporting and context could be added to a video component and delivered more immediately, to a far bigger audience.

Even in the TV medium, Gammons was something of a trailblazer. In the beginning, he lacked the standard on-camera training and was raw and unpolished. But as had happened with his newspaper career, he grew more comfortable in this new medium.

In time, he could comfortably do stand-ups from the ballpark (or the hotel lobby at the Winter Meetings) and fit in seamlessly on-set in the studio, or, as technology improved, from his own office in his Cape Cod home.

He incorporated his institutional knowledge of the game into his TV work, and watching him, you'd have never known that he had spent so long in the newspaper business. The medium may have changed, but his inexhaustible list of contacts did not, nor the goodwill that he had accumulated over his career. When Alex Rodriguez decided it was time to come clean and tell the story of his performance-enhancing drug use in 2009, he chose Gammons to conduct the interview.

Gammons continues to do TV work for MLB Network while writing for The Athletic. Neither existed even when Gammons was already decades into his career.

But sports fans continue to benefit from his knowledge and perspective, and while his national audience is greater now, his defining work will always be the years he spent at the *Globe*. It was a time when Gammons essentially invented the job of the modern beat writer and, anticipating the Information Age, wrote and wrote about topics that had gone uncovered and in a style that had not existed.

To call him the best baseball beat writer ever is to somehow understate his importance to journalism and his impact on the game of baseball.

6

Jerry Remy

In a sport in which almost everything is increasingly quantifiable, there's no reasonable measurement to measure the popularity of baseball broadcasters.

So much of it is subjective, so much of it determined by individual taste. I could like someone who I believe adds to a particular game; you, by contrast, may wonder why the same announcer "never shuts up!"

Still, it would seem pointless to argue this: Jerry Remy was the most popular Red Sox broadcaster of all time.

Certainly, he was among the longest serving in that role, working NESN telecasts from 1988 through 2021, spanning 34 seasons. Remy began his second career just 18 months after one of the most ignominious October defeats in franchise history, a time when it seemed logical to ask whether the Red Sox's championship curse would ever be broken; his final year in the booth began just 18 months after the Sox had captured their fourth title in the period of 14 years.

That's how long Remy was a fixture on Red Sox telecasts.

And it's a given that no one overcame more obstacles. On seven separate occasions, Remy battled a recurrence of cancer, returning to the booth six times. More than once, he overcame mental health issues. And famously, he dealt with a crippling tragedy within his own family.

At the very least, he was, without question, the most resilient broadcaster in the team's history.

But his career was about more than dedication to the job and overcoming adversity. Remy fulfilled the requirements of the job by making the Red Sox more entertaining, more informative, more fun.

"I'll always consider Jerry Remy the true voice of the Red Sox," said longtime play-by-play voice Dave O'Brien, who was Remy's on-air partner over the last five seasons he worked as an analyst.

That's difficult to dispute.

Prior to his career as an announcer, Remy may have had a 10-year major league career, the last seven seasons of which were spent with the Red Sox. But in many ways, he was one of us.

He was a Massachusetts native, born in Fall River and raised in nearby Somerset, and because of that geography, he *sounded* like one of us, too. He extolled the virtues of Dustin "Pedroier" and "Xandah Bogahhts," and everyone knew to whom he was referring.

If all politics is local, as Tip O'Neill once said, so, too, is baseball broadcasting, and Remy was decidedly local. His approach might not have worked in New York or the Midwest, but then, that wasn't Remy's audience.

He was well-versed in team history, in part because he had, for a time, contributed to it, having been a star player on the 1978 team that lost to the Yankees in a playoff game. He knew, firsthand, the joys of victory and the heartbreak of defeat, because he himself had experienced them. And he could provide us with the insight gleaned from playing in 1,154 major league games.

Remy's work ethic was obvious from his playing career. Chosen as an eighth-round selection by the California Angels, Remy was undersized and underpublicized. He didn't have the benefit of playing year-round, the way players from Florida or California did. He wasn't an imposing physical specimen at 5'9", 165 pounds.

He had to earn everything, which he did without complaint. He took pride in outworking players selected far higher in the draft and given far bigger signing bonuses. As a broadcaster, he would occasionally reference more celebrated players who arrived in spring training with expensive sports cars but without the discipline to become successful pro ballplayers. Remy beat a number of them to the major leagues—some never got there at all—but he would never identify those underachievers by name.

That wasn't his style.

If Remy had, in fact, a "style," it was hard work, which was imperative for someone who lacked the size and pedigree of others more physically gifted. He might not have won any strength contests among his teammates, but Remy dedicated himself to learning the game.

(His attention to detail would occasionally desert him, however. In his major league debut, he found himself being picked off first base, immediately earning the wrath of manager Dick Williams. The shame stayed with Remy for a while, though, decades later, he would retell the story frequently when a young Red Sox player suffered a similarly ignominious fate.)

His career ended prematurely at age 31 by a series of knee injuries, Remy needed a job to support himself. (Some bad financial advice and poor investments, which robbed him of much of the money saved from his playing career, made this even more imperative.) For a brief time, he tried minor league coaching, but found it wasn't for him.

Urged to apply for a vacancy in the Red Sox TV booth for NESN—a regional sports network that is 80 percent owned by the Red Sox—Remy did so, almost on a whim. To his shock, and initially his horror, he was hired.

Remy was wholly unprepared for broadcasting. He had no formal training and little guidance. In his first telecast, working with Ned Martin, Remy viewed a replay of a ground ball to short.

"There's a ground ball to short..." he noted tentatively.

In full recognition that he was—initially, at least—ill-suited for the job, Remy would later reveal that he would "pray for rainouts." He similarly dreaded Tuesdays and Fridays, when both the *Boston Globe* and *Boston Herald* would regularly run columns by TV critics, dreading more embarrassing negative feedback to his work.

Decades later, Remy, who could make self-effacement an art form, would still cringe when reviewing his TV work from his first couple of seasons.

Eventually, Remy found his voice on TV, and he arrived there by the same methods he had used as a player: repetition, preparation, and commitment.

As Remy's confidence on air grew, his deep knowledge of the game emerged and became a useful tool. But if Remy had simply analyzed a take-out slide at second or explored the intricacies of a rundown on the basepaths, he never would have become an iconic figure.

Remy's appeal was his Everyman persona—his unfailing ability to laugh at himself, to travel down off-topic rabbit holes and make midseason blowout games must-watch TV. A viewer never knew when Remy might suffer a dental mishap midsentence (he once lost a tooth in the middle of a game, prompting his longtime broadcast partner Don Orsillo to comically replace it with a pair of pliers found in the broadcast booth), or his careful reconstruction of two fans in the left field seats hurling slices at one another ("Here comes the pizza...").

As a broadcaster, as was the case during his playing career, Remy was always in a hurry. He stole 208 bases over 10 seasons. Later, that aggressiveness was on display daily.

Remy couldn't get to the ballpark fast enough. Orsillo recalled that, early in their time together, Remy would suggest meeting in the hotel lobby at 3:15 PM to grab a cab to the ballpark and be on hand when the clubhouse was opened to the media, some three and a half hours before gametime.

With each successive year, Remy moved the departure time up another 15 minutes. Maybe this was just a manifestation of his anxiety, or maybe it was just dedication to his craft. Either way, eventually, Orsillo decided to let Remy embark on his own.

(Remy's inherent need to be first, or at least to arrive early, carried into off days, too. Once, in Chicago, Remy suggested a ridiculously early dinner time, the likes of which would have been better suited for a senior citizen's "early bird special" than a high-priced Midwest steak house. When Remy arrived at the restaurant, it hadn't yet opened for dinner business, prompting him to peer into the establishment's plate glass window, like a child eager for a candy store to open. A sympathetic waiter, sensing that Remy posed no discernible danger beyond an eagerness for an early dinner, eventually unlocked the door and allowed him entry.)

At home, Remy was afforded "early bird" status into the home clubhouse. No matter how early other media members arrived, they couldn't beat Remy, who would typically pull up a chair at a table—a courtesy that would not be extended to anyone else—and begin poring over game notes and statistics.

When Remy wasn't doing traditional prep and uncovering nuggets to insert into that night's broadcast, he was conferring with coaches and players, gleaning additional insight that could prove worthwhile to viewers.

Always, there was the work, and the games, both of which sated Remy.

Of the broadcast booth, he once said, "It's always been my comfort zone."

Such an observation would have been unthinkable when Remy began in the business—nearly crippled by shyness, unsure what was expected of him or how to deliver it.

For someone who didn't grow up in New England, it might be difficult—if not impossible—to fathom just how popular Remy was, especially when the Red Sox were waging their epic battles with the Yankees and seeking their first championship in nearly nine decades.

Remy was a one-man merchandising phenomenon. His website attracted incredible traffic and anything with his name attached—including replicas of the previous night's scorecard—attracted interested buyers. At one point, his business partner, John O'Rourke, said the Remy Report website generated gross revenues of $1 million annually.

Later, a chain of sports bar restaurants bearing his name sprung up across New England, further extending his brand.

Being Jerry Remy was good for business.

However, Remy's outsize popularity was somewhat at odds with his own private persona.

By nature an introvert, Remy found fame unsettling. Just as he initially had difficulty communicating his thoughts on television, he was unprepared for his newfound celebrity. Some fans reported awkward interactions with him early in his broadcasting career, with Remy coming off as aloof and at times socially awkward.

Far from being unfriendly, Remy was simply unprepared to handle the attention and acclaim. Eventually, he grew more comfortable with the public side of his career and came to recognize that the outpouring of affection was merely a manifestation of his appeal. Even though fans had no personal history with Remy, they *felt* a connection. After all, wasn't he a guest in their living rooms on a nightly basis for six months running? Hadn't he shared with them a devotion to the Red Sox?

In the last decade of his life, Remy's private battles with cancer, his mental health, and his son Jared's criminality became public and stripped Remy of any armor. There was no "private" Jerry Remy anymore; it was all, like it or not, very much on display.

Remy confronted his health struggles—physical and mental—head-on in interviews and speaking engagements, urging anyone who was listening to get cancer screenings and to not be ashamed to ask for help when it came to depression. He had fought these fights publicly and used his platform of celebrity to do the same.

His son's arrest for murder in 2013—and subsequent admission of guilt—was his most difficult battle. After Jared was charged with murdering his girlfriend, Jennifer Martel, the mother of his daughter, it was reported that he had had several interactions with law enforcement over the years, and that his father had interceded on his behalf, asking for leniency with his son.

While some fans said this made Jerry at least somewhat culpable for Martel's death, most understood that he was merely doing what many parents would have in the same situation by attempting to help his son.

"Did we enable him?" Remy asked rhetorically in an interview with WEEI Radio. "Yes, we paid for lawyers. We paid for psychiatrists. We paid for the help we thought he needed."

Jared Remy pleaded guilty and was sentenced to life without parole. The elder Remy, after taking some time away from the booth, returned the next spring—dealing with both grief and guilt. Initially, he was met with resistance from once-loyal viewers, some of whom thought it inappropriate that Remy had returned to work and was again providing commentary.

But in time, those objections seemed to dissipate. His own battles—repeatedly with cancer and occasionally with his own mental health—interrupted his work, with Remy taking periodic absences from the job. Always, however, he had fans wishing him well in whatever it was that had sidelined him.

In the last weeks of his life, Remy made one final public appearance, arriving at Fenway Park as a surprise guest to throw out the first pitch prior to the Red Sox's wild-card playoff game against their archrivals, the New York Yankees.

He arrived on the field in a bullpen cart, waving to fans who stood and applauded. When he emerged from the cart near the pitcher's mound, his appearance was shocking: gaunt and weakened by endless rounds of chemotherapy, he was on oxygen, with an extra-long breathing tube to provide him with a modicum of maneuverability.

His movements were unsteady and there was little oomph to his throw, caught by once-teammate and broadcast partner Dennis Eckersley. As the two embraced in front of the mound,

Eckersley told Remy that he loved him, and—gesturing to the ovation from the stands—so did everyone in attendance.

As Remy absorbed the outpouring of emotion, it was hard to watch it all unfold and not think that this was a goodbye of sorts. Watching Remy circle the ballpark on the warning track from inside the bullpen cart proved to be a highly emotional prelude to an already highly anticipated showdown with the Yankees.

Remy had vowed—privately to friends and publicly in statements released by NESN—to fight the latest recurrence of cancer with the same vigor he exhibited in his six previous battles. But there's a limit to the body's ability to battle such an insidious disease, and this round proved too much. Less than a month later, he passed away, a week shy of his 69th birthday.

His death marked the end of an era for the Red Sox and their broadcast booth. In his career as an analyst he partnered with Bob Kurtz, Ned Martin, Sean McDonough, Don Orsillo, and Dave O'Brien. Even with his health-related absences, he was, effectively, the one constant of Red Sox telecasts from 1989 to 2021, a period that spanned generations.

In his first year in the booth, Remy analyzed games featuring former teammates (Jim Rice, Wade Boggs, Dwight Evans, Rich Gedman, Marty Barrett, and Bob Stanley); in his final season, most of the players on the 2021 Red Sox hadn't been born when Remy began his broadcasting career. Some were young enough to be Remy's grandchildren.

That Remy's appeal would stretch out over decades and across generations was only fitting. He cut across the years, connecting with some fans who had watched his playing career and still others who might have been unaware that he ever occupied a spot in the Fenway infield.

In his later years, when he was absent because of cancer or his mental health battles, viewers offered well wishes and prayers for his return to good health, and to the telecasts.

Over the years, a number of former Red Sox players—including Mel Parnell, Johnny Pesky, Rico Petrocelli, Ken Harrelson, Mike Andrews, Bob Montgomery, and Eckersley—worked radio or TV broadcasts as analysts. Some had enjoyed better playing careers; some were perhaps more polished broadcasters.

But it's safe to say that none resonated as deeply with the fan base as did Remy, whose time in the TV booth coincided with the most successful era of the franchise and whose descriptions of and reactions to those magic moments will live with Red Sox fans for a long, long time.

PART 3

THE RIVALRY

7

The Yankees Dominate (1920–1977)

IN REAL LIFE, CHICAGO LONG AGO EARNED THE NICKNAME the "Second City." In sports, for the longest time, that sobriquet might better be applied to Boston.

From some 200 or so miles away, Boston has always been the younger sibling to New York's Big Brother. New York is known as the "Big City." Boston, by contrast, is often referred to as a "town"—smaller, less intimidating, perhaps. At least in theory.

New York's reputation is that of a bigger, faster, more hectic environment, with a population base more than 10 times its distant cousin to the northeast. New York has Wall Street, Broadway, and Times Square; Boston has "districts"—financial and theater—but its reach and influence are far more modest.

To many Bostonians, New York represents excess. It's bigger, louder, more expensive, while Boston is more modest and manageable. They can cede New York the edge in finance, fashion, and culture.

But sports supremacy is another matter.

There are some things Boston can abide. Losing to a team from New York is not among them.

If one transaction could come to represent the animosity Boston feels toward New York, it's undoubtedly the sale of Babe Ruth to the Yankees in 1919.

In all of sports, no single player movement has ever impacted two franchises as dramatically and for as long as this one did.

To this day, it may be hard even for die-hard Red Sox fans to appreciate the dominance of their franchise in the first two decades of the 20th century. From 1903, two years after their inception, through 1918, the Red Sox—or their antecedents, the Boston Americans—captured five World Series, more than any other team in either league.

Four of those titles came in the span of seven seasons, making those Red Sox baseball's first dynasty.

Then came the infamous sale of Ruth to the Yankees, and with it, the balance of power seemed to shift almost instantly.

Before Ruth's arrival, the Yankees—or their forebears—never won an American League pennant, much less a World Series. And after he arrived? The Yankees emerged a baseball powerhouse. Within two years, they had made their first visit to the Series. By 1932, they had made seven trips, winning four.

The Yankee juggernaut was underway, and the franchise had the Red Sox to thank.

There was no turning back now. From 1936 through 1943, with Ruth having left the Yankees, retired, and later, passed away, the Yankees won seven pennants and six World Series.

It would continue throughout the 1940s and 1950s, with the winning so regular and the team so dominant that a season in which the Yankees didn't at least get to the Fall Classic felt like something of an aberration.

All the while, the Red Sox, while star-driven, were utter failures when it came to team accomplishments. From 1919 to 1966, a 47-year stretch, the Red Sox won exactly one (1) American League pennant and no World Series.

It wasn't as though the Sox lacked star power. There was Ted Williams, of course, only the greatest hitter in the game's history. And he was occasionally augmented by Jimmie Foxx, Bobby Doerr, and other greats.

But always, it seemed, the Red Sox lacked the necessary pitching to be among the best teams in the game.

While the Red Sox couldn't begin to match the Yankees' postseason success, the relative proximity of the two franchises resulted in a natural rivalry. Yes, the Yankees shared New York City with the Dodgers in Brooklyn and the Giants in Manhattan and would square off against both in some epic World Series meetings.

But it was the Red Sox who by dint of geography filled the role of American League rival.

If the Red Sox couldn't begin to match the Yankees in terms of team success, the rivalry, especially in the 1940s, focused on the teams' most identifiable stars—Williams for the Red Sox and Joe DiMaggio for the Yanks.

Both transcended the game, though for varied reasons.

DiMaggio was known as the best player on the most famous team in America, and that was enough to establish him as perhaps the most popular athlete in the country.

While Williams was the better hitter, DiMaggio was certainly the more complete player—graceful in the outfield and instinctive on the basepaths. If his home run total was modest—361 over 13 seasons—that could be attributed at least in part to the hitting environment in which he competed.

The old Yankee Stadium featured an absurdly deep left-center field area that robbed DiMaggio of countless homers. Over the course of his career, DiMaggio never once hit a single homer at Yankee Stadium between the power alleys, stretching from left-center to right-center.

But if DiMaggio was never exclusively a power hitter—he hit more than 30 homers just five times—he was a skilled one. An expert in putting the ball in play with a fearsome line drive swing, he finished with just eight more strikeouts than he had homers. In the 1941 season, in which he hit in 56 consecutive games, DiMaggio fanned just 13 times in 541 at-bats. (In the modern game, a player might accumulate 13 strikeouts in a four-game series.)

DiMaggio may have been the Yankees' top star, but he was hardly alone. While Williams was surrounded by other All-Stars, DiMaggio played with a handful of other Hall of Famers: Yogi Berra, Bill Dickey, Tony Lazzeri, Phil Rizzuto, Red Ruffing, Lefty Gomez, Joe Gordon, and Lou Gehrig all gained entrance into Cooperstown after being teammates of DiMaggio's.

Throughout this time, the teams may have been separated by only 200 or so miles on the map, but in the American League standings, the Yankees could have been forgiven if they barely noticed the Red Sox.

Consider that from 1940 to 1951, the last dozen years of DiMaggio's career, the Yankees won the American League pennant seven times while the Red Sox won just once (1946).

On two other occasions, the Red Sox came close. They dropped a one-game playoff to Cleveland in 1948. The following season, the Red Sox again came agonizingly close.

The Sox led the Yankees by a game with two games remaining in 1949 before heading to the Bronx for a season-ending two-game series. Just one win in the final two games would have given the Red Sox their second AL pennant in the span of four years.

Despite being without DiMaggio (heel injury) for the first half of the season, the Yankees led the league most of the way before the Red Sox executed a come-from-behind vault over New York in the standings in the final week of the season. On September 25, the Sox occupied first place for the first time that year after taking three in a row from the Yankees.

In the first game, the Red Sox raced to a 4–0 lead after just three innings while chasing Allie Reynolds. But the Yankees chipped away against Sox ace lefty Mel Parnell, with two runs in the fourth before adding two more in the fifth to tie the game.

A solo homer by Johnny Lindell in the bottom of the eighth gave the Yankees their first lead of the afternoon, and in the ninth, New York reliever Joe Page turned back the Sox in order, securing the victory.

Heading into the final day of the season, the teams had identical records, making the last game on the schedule effectively a playoff contest for the right to represent the American League in the World Series.

A brilliant pitching duel ensued between the Red Sox's Ellis Kinder, a 20-game winner, and the Yankees' Vic Raschi. For seven innings, the only run from either team came when Rizzuto led off the home half of the first with a triple before scoring on an infield groundout.

In the bottom of the eighth, the two teams had combined for just five hits—two by the Sox, three for the Yankees—before the Yanks erupted.

Parnell, who had started the previous game, was Joe McCarthy's curious choice to pitch the eighth. That move, predictably, blew up in the manager's face. Tommy Henrich homered. Tex Hughson entered and got DiMaggio to hit into a double play, but New York then loaded the bases and Jerry Coleman emptied them with a three-run double to right.

Gamely, the Sox attempted to rally in the ninth. A two-run triple by Doerr and a run-scoring single by Billy Goodman brought the Sox to within two runs and brought Birdie Tebbetts to the plate, representing the potential tying run. But the threat ended as Tebbetts fouled out to first, and the Yankees were crowned league champions.

Making matters worse was the fact that Williams, who collected just one hit in five official at-bats in the series, lost out on the American League batting title by a fraction to Detroit's George Kell—.34276 to Kell's .34291. That, in turn, prevented Williams from winning what would have been his third Triple Crown.

If the 1940s were full of a few close calls for the Sox, the 1950s offered no such consolation. Though DiMaggio retired at just 36 after the 1951 season, the Yankees would be no less dominant. Beginning in 1950 and stretching through 1959, the Yankees would win eight more pennants (and six more World Series). Twice in that stretch, the Yanks won four pennants in succession.

In contrast, after being highly competitive in the latter half of the 1940s, the Sox were the very definition of mediocre in the 1950s. The best they could manage was four third-place finishes, but even that proved illusory—after a 94-win season in 1950, for the remainder of the decade, the Sox were double-digit games out of first in every other season that decade.

After winning five straight additional pennants from 1960 to 1964—and two more World Series to boot—the Yankees' long era of dominance finally ground to a halt. From 1965 through 1975, the Yankees didn't win another pennant, which, for their fan base, must have seemed like an eternity.

The Yankees, who had only integrated four years before the Red Sox did, began to pay the price for not developing more Black players. At the same time, many of the stars who had helped them to dominate in the 1950s began to age out or deal with injuries. After 1964, Mickey Mantle, his knees ravaged, was a shell of himself.

In the mid-1960s, the Yankees were barely recognizable. Horace Clarke, Jake Gibbs, and others were hardly worthy heirs to the immortals who preceded them.

Not that the Red Sox were positioned to take advantage of this dip by their rivals. Williams' retirement in 1960 helped usher in a period in which the Sox were seldom competitive. In fact, a case could be made that 1961–67 was the single-worst six-year stretch in franchise history. Not even expansion—the American League expanded from eight teams to 10 in 1961—could help the hapless Sox, who, in that span, finished an *average* of 32 games out of first.

The 1967 season, meanwhile, saw the Sox begin a new era of competitiveness. Whether coincidentally or not, it also ignited some on-field tensions between the rivals.

It took a quick response from Jim Lonborg, who would go on to win the Cy Young Award that season, to spark things. On June 21, Yankee pitcher Thad Tillotson struck Sox third baseman Joe Foy in the helmet with a pitch. In retaliation, in the bottom of the inning, Lonborg drilled Tillotson between the shoulder blades, a not-unexpected response.

Much jawing between the principals ensued. Sox shortstop Rico Petrocelli and Yankee first baseman Joe Pepitone—from the same New York neighborhood but having attended rival high schools—were the principals, and before long, both dugouts and bullpens emptied. Among the dozen or so cops coming into the field to restore order was Petrocelli's brother.

Still things weren't settled. When Tillotson fired a pitch aimed at Reggie Smith's ankles a couple of innings later, Lonborg decided he wasn't done settling the score. In the next inning, and just for good measure, he hit Dick Howser.

It was the first on-field brawl between the teams in a long time, but by no means would it be the last.

Even though neither team won much of anything for the next seven years, the heat was turned up.

In 1973, the teams' catchers, Carlton Fisk and Thurman Munson, came to symbolize the dislike the two sides had for one another. Munson felt overlooked and harbored some resentment of the attention Fisk, the AL Rookie of the Year the previous season, had received.

On August 1, that ill will came to a head. Munson barreled into Fisk on a squeeze play, and the two came up swinging, with Gene Michael, the batter at the time, joining in. Bill Lee, who fancied himself an iconoclast, joked to *Sports Illustrated* that watching Michael and Munson was like watching "two hookers fighting on 45th Street."

That eruption, as it turned out, was a mere precursor to a famed brawl in 1976, which had far greater consequences.

New York outfielder Lou Piniella attempted to score from second on a single to right, but a strike from Dwight Evans beat Piniella to the plate. Fisk caught the throw and was immediately bowled over by the hard-charging Piniella. The catcher held on to the ball, resulting in an out, but unhappy with Piniella's aggressive slide, he came up swinging at the baserunner, touching off a giant melee.

As Piniella and Fisk exchanged blows, Lee raced to home plate to aid his catcher. But he was soon intercepted by Graig Nettles, who body-slammed Lee to the ground, resulting in a separated shoulder that would sideline the quirky lefty for much of the remainder of the season.

Circling the pile of humanity was New York outfielder Mickey Rivers, who proved expert at launching rabbit punches at defenseless Sox players, then scurrying away before being detected.

When Lee finally extricated himself, his left shoulder conspicuously caved in, he went seeking revenge from Nettles, who promptly supplied the finishing touch with one more jab to the face, leaving Lee with a black eye, to say nothing of a severely damaged wing and bruised ego.

Nettles had long ago expressed regret that Lee had incurred considerable damage to his shoulder. But he felt no such guilt over the shiner that he supplied.

"He just tried to sneak around the pile," Nettles recalled, decades later, to the *Hartford Courant*, "and he came at me, getting in my face, so, again, I wanted to make sure he wasn't hit with any purse."

It was a reminder that, in this era, players didn't forget—even from an on-field incident three years earlier.

As for the rivalry, these were mere warm-ups to the Main Event of 1978. That season didn't include any fisticuffs, but it would feature one of the most compelling and unpredictable pennant races the game had ever seen.

8

1978

THOUGH THEY STILL HAD NO WORLD CHAMPIONSHIPS TO their credit, the Red Sox of the mid- to late 1970s could at least make the case that they had become competitive with their rivals—which was more than they could say about the previous couple of decades.

The Yankees still ruled with a pennant in 1976 and a World Series title in 1977, their first after a 14-year championship drought. The Red Sox had only the 1975 pennant—and their oh-so-close defeat to the Cincinnati Reds—of which to boast, but it was something, at least.

And even in the seasons in which they failed to reach the postseason, the Red Sox were relevant. They mattered, which is more than could be said for long stretches in the 1960s and 1970s, while the Yankees added one ring after another.

Consider:

In 1974, the Red Sox were in first place as September began before going 12–19 the rest of the way and dropping into third place in the American League East.

In 1975, they won the pennant, swept the defending champion Oakland A's in the ALCS, and reached Game 7 of the World Series.

In 1977, the Sox held first place for good chunks of the first five months of the season before settling for 97 wins and a second-place finish behind the Yanks.

As the next season began, they had won 95 or more games in two of the previous three seasons and there was reason to believe—hope!—that 1978 would again see them challenging for the division title.

The 1978 Red Sox were an offensive powerhouse, led by a trio of homegrown outfielders, each in his prime. Jim Rice, Fred Lynn, and Dwight Evans would combine for 92 homers, and Rice would have the best Red Sox season since Carl Yastrzemski—still contributing at 38—won the Triple Crown in 1967.

Rice would be the first American League hitter since Joe DiMaggio in 1937 to collect 400 or more (406) total bases in a season and would be chosen as the 1978 AL MVP.

Even the Red Sox pitching was improved. Days before the season started, the team acquired Dennis Eckersley, a young, brash righthander from Cleveland, who would lead the staff with 20 wins. Mike Torrez, swiped from the Yankees the previous offseason in one of the club's first forays into the burgeoning free agent market, would contribute 16 wins and 250 innings. Ageless Luis Tiant, operating at 37, was good for 31 starts, 13 victories, and a more than respectable 3.31 ERA.

Under manager Don Zimmer, on the job for his second full season after replacing the fired Darrell Johnson in 1976, the Red Sox proved to be the class of the division in the first half.

Zimmer was as old-school as they come, with a giant wad of chewing tobacco that seemed surgically and permanently implanted in his cheek, giving his already round face a more comical appearance, and earning him the nickname "Popeye."

To suggest that Zimmer was a baseball lifer would be to understate his commitment to the game. From 1949 to his passing in 2014, Zimmer was employed in baseball in some capacity or another—player, coach, or manager—for 65 uninterrupted years. The game's influence on his identity was so strong that he married his high school sweetheart Carol (known to all as "Soot") in 1951 in a ceremony at home plate prior to a minor league game in Elmira, New York.

Zimmer had been a member of the famed Brooklyn Dodgers teams in the 1950s but had to overcome being struck in the temple by a pitch in the minor leagues in 1953, which left him unconscious for nearly two weeks. The injury was life-threatening and helped lead to the mandated use of protective batting helmets.

After his playing career, he managed the San Diego Padres for two seasons before joining the Boston staff as Johnson's third base coach.

Managing in the cauldron that is Boston, Zimmer had little use for second-guessing and would react harshly to criticism at times. Despite that, Zimmer would listen to sports talk radio on his way to and from the ballpark and grew so frustrated by the abuse he took from one show, the *Sports Huddle,* that he issued an unofficial cease-and-desist order to the show's hosts, demanding that they never mention his name.

(The hosts, playing along, complied and, for a time, developed a code name for the manager of the local baseball team: Chiang Kai-Shek.)

Zimmer's style was to trust the players, especially the veterans, and, for the most part, stay out of the way. In his first two seasons, he had engendered the formation of a group of players who called themselves the Buffalo Heads, counterculture adherents united in their dislike for Zimmer's ultraconservatism.

The group included Bernie Carbo, Ferguson Jenkins, Rick Wise, Jim Willoughby, Dick Pole, Allen Ripley, and, of course, Bill Lee. By 1978, only Ripley and Lee remained, and Zimmer did his best to ignore both—to the team's detriment in the fateful final month of the season.

Aside from the difficulty he had in relating to younger, more irreverent players, if Zimmer had a fault as a manager, it was his habit of playing his regulars to the point of exhaustion. In 1978, Carlton Fisk may have been the game's best catcher, but Zimmer was reluctant to give him any time off, inserting him into the starting lineup in all but a dozen games.

Five of the team's nine regulars totaled more than 600 plate appearances and two others topped 570. Though beloved by many of the veteran players, Zimmer was a no-nonsense taskmaster who expected his regulars to play day after day after day.

This proved disastrous in at least one case. Zimmer continued to run Butch Hobson out to third base, despite the presence of nagging bone chips in Hobson's right elbow. Hobson could be seen readjusting the bone chips in his elbow joint between pitches, which doubtless contributed to his absurdly high error total of 43, many of them on wild throws to first. A tough-as-nails Alabaman who had played college football for

Bear Bryant, Hobson was too proud to ask out of the lineup, and Zimmer was too stubborn to replace him.

Still, for all the roster imperfections, the Sox flew to a comfortable cruising altitude in the first half. At the All-Star break, the Sox led second-place Milwaukee by nine full games and third-place New York by 11.5. They were almost unbeatable at home, too, winning an astounding 34 of their first 40 home games.

Given their penchant for second-half slippage in recent seasons, the division title could not be considered wrapped up with another two and a half months remaining on the schedule.

But at the very least, the Red Sox had a firm grasp of the division.

"We were on top of the world," Eckersley would recall nearly 40 years later.

Or so it seemed.

Meanwhile, all was not well with the Yankees. The defending champs, who had won the previous two pennants, were an internal mess, full of personality clashes, power grabs, and ego trips. When Reggie Jackson defied combustible manager Billy Martin's orders and tried to bunt in the ninth inning, owner George Steinbrenner suspended his star slugger for five games.

Martin found this suspension to be lenient and when Jackson returned, claiming he had done nothing wrong, Martin was further incensed. Referencing his owner's prior felony for illegal contributions, Martin, emboldened as he often was with a few drinks, famously said of Jackson and Steinbrenner, "One's a born liar; the other's convicted."

That was it for Martin, who was dismissed and replaced by Bob Lemon, who himself had been fired by the White Sox only a month earlier. Lemon was everything Martin was not—unassuming and far from confrontational.

He told his new charges, "You guys won last year. So why don't you go out and play the way you did last year, and I'll try to stay the hell out of the way."

The change in the dugout proved the perfect elixir for the Yankees, who, freed from Martin's overbearing manner and without the Billy versus George sideshow, began to play up to their pedigree, winning 17 of their first 25 games under the more taciturn Lemon.

At the same time, the Sox began to run out of gas. Defensive lapses and regression from the pitching corps saw the Sox begin to lose altitude.

Injuries and a lack of depth combined to deliver a one-two punch to the Sox. Shortstop Rick Burleson was lost for nearly three weeks with an ankle injury and the Sox went 6–12 in his absence. A wrist injury to Jerry Remy in late August proved costly, too. Yastrzemski and Fisk, meanwhile, played through painful, nagging injuries that limited them—a testament to their toughness, yes, but also a reflection of the team's inadequate depth.

Career journeymen like Fred Kendall, Frank Duffy, and Jack Brohamer weren't going to save the day.

By mid-August, the Sox's once impenetrable lead in the division had been shaved down to five games, and when the Yankees arrived for a key four-game showdown series at Fenway just after Labor Day, the lead had been whittled to just four.

Not for long.

The Yankees unloaded on Red Sox pitching, sweeping the series and outscoring the humbled Sox by a margin of 42–9. The Sox, suddenly, could do nothing right. They hit just .171 for the series; worse, the Sox were seemingly intent on handing the games to the Yankees, committing an unfathomable dozen errors in the field.

In the first game of the series, after the Yankees had raced out to a 7–0 lead in the first three innings, a lasting image remained. It showed a disconsolate Carl Yastrzemski slumped against the left field wall during a pitching change, emblematic of his team's frustration.

In the finale, Zimmer, ever stubborn, passed over Lee for a start and instead gave the ball to rookie Bobby Sprowl, making his second big-league appearance. Sprowl appeared for all the world to be having a nervous breakdown on the mound, issuing four walks to the first six hitters he faced. He was then lifted without completing the first inning, setting in motion the sweep by the Yanks.

The once safe lead was soon gone, and for the rest of September, the Sox were in the unenviable position of playing from behind, forced to chase the Yankees after having played the role of division leaders for most of the first five months of the season.

To their credit, after dropping two more games to the Yankees in New York a week later, the Sox got off the mat. Trailing by 3.5 games with 14 games left, the Sox went 12–2 down the stretch to forge a tie on the final game of the season.

Their comeback will never get the full recognition it deserves, coming as it did following the team's historic collapse. But it would have been easy for the Sox to fold after first place was ceded to their rivals. Criticize them all you like for blowing the 14-game cushion over the Yanks, but remember, too, the toughness and resilience they displayed to come back and forge the one-game playoff.

The Sox won the coin flip for home field for the "playoff game"—in actuality, it was considered Game No. 163, an extension of the regular season—which was held on Monday, October 2.

Prior to the game, Jackson summed up the atmosphere perfectly.

"The season coming down to a game like this, between them and us, is kind of perfect," he said. "I mean, where else would you want to be today?"

But there was trepidation, too, perhaps reflected in the different histories experienced by the two franchises. The Yankees were accustomed to happy endings. The Red Sox? Not so much.

"I had never been more nervous before a game in my life," said Eckersley. "And I didn't even pitch."

It was a sunny, crisp autumn day, and it seemed fitting that the game was played in the afternoon, like so many historic games between the rivals in the past had been.

The Sox grabbed an early lead on a solo homer from Yaz in the second and added to it in the sixth on a run-scoring single from Rice. Torrez limited his former team to just two hits and no runs over the first six innings.

It seemed too easy. And it was.

In the seventh, singles by Graig Nettles and Chris Chambliss set the stage for light-hitting shortstop Bucky Dent, who turned on a pitch from Torrez and sent it into the screen atop the Green Monster. Yastrzemski, who knew a thing or two about his home ballpark's dimensions after almost 20 seasons, turned around and up, in the futile hope that the ball would be coming back to him. It did not.

An RBI double from Thurman Munson later that inning and a solo homer by Jackson in the eighth stretched the lead to 5–2.

Still, the Sox didn't fold. Just as they had done in the final two weeks of the regular season, they gamely clawed back. After Jerry Remy doubled, Yastrzemski singled him home and consecutive singles from Lynn and Fisk delivered Yaz as the Sox got back to within a run.

In the ninth, fate intervened—and not in a good way for the home team.

Following a leadoff walk by Rick Burleson, Remy hit a line drive to right that New York outfielder Lou Piniella lost in the air. Piniella was blinded by the combination of late afternoon shadows and sun and couldn't see the ball as it neared him. Ever resourceful, he never showed any panic, sticking out his glove at the last possible moment. Remarkably, the ball bounced in front of Piniella and found its way into his glove, as if attracted by a magnet.

"I never saw it," conceded Piniella after the game. "I just said, 'Don't panic. Don't wave your damn arms and let the runner know you've lost it.' It was just pure luck that I could get my glove on the ball. If it had gone to the wall, those two scooters would still be running around the bases."

Instead of Burleson taking third, where he would have represented the tying run with one out and from where he could have easily scored on Rice's flyout that followed, he had to be content to stay at second.

That meant the Sox were down to the final out, with hard-throwing closer Goose Gossage matched against, fittingly, Yastrzemski. Here was the captain's chance. Here, finally, was an opportunity to make amends for making the final out in the 1975 World Series.

"It's like the script was written for him," said Remy.

Instead, Yastrzemski hit a pop-up into foul territory near third and Nettles, in the shadows, snared the ball and snuffed out the Red Sox's hopes for good.

In the clubhouse afterward, Yastrzemski meticulously recounted the final at-bat for wave after wave of reporters.

He had hoped to drive a fastball from Gossage into right field, delivering Burleson and extending the season for, at minimum, one more inning.

Instead, the pitch jackknifed in on his hands and the aging legend took a more defensive swing, resulting in a harmless pop-up.

Fighting back tears, Yastrzemski wondered aloud, to himself, as much as anyone else, "You wonder if it's meant to be."

It wasn't clear to which he was specifically referring—that at-bat? Beating the Yankees? Winning a World Series?

But the net effect of the remark was the same. Once more, the Red Sox had come up empty-handed. That it came in a season in which they appeared so firmly in control for so long, right up until the third-to-last inning of the final game of the season, made it sting that much more.

Naturally, the Yankees, buoyed by their winner-take-all victory that afternoon, went on to defeat the Kansas City Royals for the pennant, then took down the Los Angeles Dodgers for their second championship in a row.

Meanwhile, the Sox—and their fans—were left shell-shocked. If not this year, they wondered, then when?

Would a lead—any lead—ever feel safe again? Would the Sox shake the ignominy of the worst collapse in modern baseball history?

Not for a long time, as it turned out. The seasons that followed saw the Sox border on irrelevant. A 91-win season got them no better than third place in the division and cost Zimmer his job. For the next five seasons thereafter, the Sox were a study in mediocrity, their organization plagued by an ugly ownership squabble while star player after star player—Fisk, Lynn, Burleson—was either traded or lost via free agency.

The Yankees didn't just defeat the Red Sox in that one-game showdown; they left them with a multiyear hangover.

The Sox wouldn't reach the postseason again for almost another decade, and before they could exact some revenge against the Yankees, they would need to suffer one more cruel October defeat at their hands.

It may have seemed unimaginable at the time, but that one would be every bit as painful as the last.

9

2003

It's easy to forget now, but there was a period—and not too long ago—when the New York Yankees weren't the Red Sox's most obvious rival.

As had happened between 1964 and 1976, the Yankees went into a fallow period following their 1981 World Series loss to the Los Angeles Dodgers—the third meeting between the former New York neighbors in the span of five seasons—and didn't return to contention until 1995.

As was the case in the mid-1960s through the mid-1970s, the playoff drought felt like an eternity for Yankee fans who had come to expect that trips to the postseason were a birthright. But by the early 1980s, owner George Steinbrenner's impetuous moves—trading off prospects, firing managers on a whim, and his general overbearing, meddlesome presence—had the effect of scarring his famed franchise and impeding its progress.

It was hardly a coincidence that the Yankees' climb back to relevance began when Steinbrenner was in exile, banned from the game by commissioner Fay Vincent for his association with noted gambler Howie Spira. In Steinbrenner's absence, cooler heads prevailed. Gene Michael, more patient and stressing the importance of player development, oversaw the Yanks' return to glory.

At the same time, the Red Sox, in the aftermath of their heartbreaking loss in the 1986 World Series, began a period in which they were revitalized. The team won division titles in 1988 and 1990 and were a half-game back in 1991 in late September before a major nosedive in 1991 left them seven games in back and left manager Joe Morgan as the scapegoat and out of a job.

From the late 1980s through the late 1990s, the Red Sox found themselves in the unique position of giving the Yankees little thought. They were instead consumed by the Oakland A's, who twice vanquished them in the ALCS, and for a time, in their own division, by the Toronto Blue Jays, whom they beat out by two games in 1990, then fell behind in 1991.

And it was the Jays who captured consecutive World Series in 1992–93 before the strike wiped out the 1994 Fall Classic. Suddenly, the American League East had a new standard-bearer and the model franchise operated from north of the border.

The Yankees? They were an afterthought, too dysfunctional with whom to be concerned. For a change, it was the Yankees—and not the snake-bitten Red Sox—who served as their own worst enemies.

When the A's and Jays weren't the object of the Red Sox's desires, Cleveland emerged as a rival of sorts in the mid-1990s. It was Cleveland who dismissed the Sox without so much as a drop of sweat in 1995, the first year of MLB's expanded playoff format,

Cleveland, which had been building toward contender status for several years, arrived fully formed in 1995 and swept the Sox three straight before advancing to the World Series. The 1998 season ended with the same familiar thud as it had three years previous—with the club merely toying with the Sox, this time in four games. Cleveland won the AL pennant in 1995 and again in 1997.

Meanwhile, the sleeping monster in the Bronx had awoken. The Yankees had won the World Series in 1996, and, after taking care of Cleveland in 1998, won it again.

In 1999, the bitter antagonists were on a collision course. The Red Sox, seemingly headed for a third first-round loss to Cleveland in the span of five years, rallied to defeat them at Jacobs Field in a winner-take-all Game 5 while the Yankees were making quick work of the Texas Rangers.

For the first time since 1978, the Yankees and Red Sox would meet with an advancement in the postseason on the line. This matchup, however, presented little drama, with the Yankees easily dispatching the Sox in five games in the ALCS.

There was no drama this time, no victory snatched away at the last minute. The Red Sox were simply not in the Yanks' class, and it showed.

Things were changing in Boston, however. The sale of the team—in between the 2001 and 2002 seasons—seemed to introduce a sense of urgency to the franchise. In 2002, the Sox showed progress, winning 93 games, but still finished double figures behind the Yankees in the loss column.

In December 2002, the Red Sox had a vibrant, young general manager running the team in the person of Theo Epstein. Enabled by new owner John Henry's checkbook and the owner's commitment to end his new franchise's title drought, then entering its ninth decade, Epstein set about trying to overtake the Yanks.

The two franchises each focused their resources on former Cuban star Jose Contreras, who had defected from the island nation and established residency in Nicaragua. Epstein traveled to Central America to engage in a bidding war for the 31-year-old righthander.

The Sox felt they were well-positioned to win the auction, but at the last minute, Contreras' affections shifted, and he chose the Yankees' offer instead. Legend has it—though long denied by Epstein—that the young Sox executive took out his frustration on some hotel room furniture.

Team president and CEO Larry Lucchino lamented the power of the pinstripes.

"The Evil Empire extends its tentacles even into Latin America," said Lucchino.

Evil Empire? Oh, the Rivalry was back, all right.

The 2003 Red Sox were an offensive juggernaut, scoring a staggering 961 runs. Six different Red Sox hitters belted more than 25 homers. Eight of the nine regulars in the lineup amassed 85 RBI. Four hitters had an OPS of .938 or greater.

The Sox were such a powerhouse at the plate that nearly one of every four games that season resulted in the Red Sox winning by five runs or more.

Even the rotation was surprisingly good. Derek Lowe won 17 games to pace the staff and while his 4.47 ERA seems bloated in retrospect, this was the height of the PED era, when offense was at its peak. (The league average ERA that season was 4.52, and only two AL teams that season finished under 4.00 as a staff.)

What the Red Sox lacked, however, was a suitable bullpen and that would, indirectly, prove their undoing at season's end.

During the regular season, the Red Sox nipped at the Yankees' heels, trailing most of the race while keeping them within reach. In the first week of September, the Sox had narrowed the deficit to just a game and a half in the division, but the Yankees showed an impressive finishing kick and pulled away down the stretch, taking the East by six games.

Still, at a time when teams in the same division couldn't meet in the division series, it seemed obvious that the clubs were on a collision course.

To fulfill their Manifest Destiny, the Red Sox first had to rid themselves of the pesky Oakland A's in the division series. When Oakland won the first two games, the Sox had that sinking feeling. But they rallied bravely and took the next two at home—one in extra innings—forcing a decisive Game 5 back in Oakland.

Homers by Manny Ramirez and Jason Varitek in the sixth produced four runs and (barely) stood up, with Derek Lowe escaping a bases-loaded jam in the bottom of the ninth to preserve the win.

With the Yankees limiting the overmatched Minnesota Twins to six runs in four games in the other division series, the two teams were positioned, for the second time in five years, for a head-on collision in the ALCS. This time, the Red Sox were far better equipped for the meeting.

The clubs split the first two games, both relatively nondescript. But when the series shifted back to Boston, things got interesting in a hurry.

The game featured a pitching matchup for the ages, with a former Red Sox ace (Roger Clemens) pitted against the present one (Pedro Martinez).

Martinez buzzed New York outfielder Karim Garcia in the top of the fourth, enraging the Yankees. In apparent retribution,

Clemens came up-and-in to Manny Ramirez, who overreacted to the location of the pitch and approached Clemens in a threatening manner.

As the benches emptied, Don Zimmer, a still-feisty 72-year-old, lunged toward Martinez like a bull. Forced into playing the reluctant matador, Martinez sidestepped the oncoming Zimmer and flung him aside, sending the coach to the ground, face-first.

Other than suffering a minor cut to his face, Zimmer was unharmed. But the hostilities had changed the tenor of the series for good.

"We've upgraded from a battle to a war," said Boston manager Grady Little in his trademark southern drawl.

Back and forth the series went, with the Sox taking Game 4 to even the series before dropping Game 5 as the ALCS returned to New York.

In Game 6, the Sox blew an early four-run lead, with the Yankees scoring four in the fourth and going up by a run in the fifth. But in a delicious bit of payback, the Sox put up a three-spot off Contreras in the seventh to take the lead for good, then added two more in the ninth for good measure in a 9–6 victory.

Through six games, it was all even, setting up a thrilling Game 7.

Once more, the Red Sox raced out front in the early going, leading 4–0 in the fifth. Wasn't this always the way?

In 1975, they had led midway through Game 7 of the World Series...and lost.

In 1978, they had led midway through the one-game playoff…and lost.

In 1986, they had led midway through Game 7 of the World Series...and lost.

Now, they led again. But as if adhering to a script, the Yanks notched a run in the fifth and another in the seventh—both coming on solo homers from Jason Giambi—cutting the Boston margin in half.

In the eighth, David Ortiz homered, giving him his eighth RBI of the series, and padding the Sox lead to three. But in the bottom of the inning, Martinez was clearly showing signs of fatigue. First came a one-out double by Derek Jeter, followed by a run-scoring single by Bernie Williams.

A third straight hit—a double from Hideki Matsui—gave the Yankees two runners in scoring position and brought Little to the mound. Everyone in the ballpark expected Martinez to get the hook. But the only man empowered to make that decision decided otherwise.

When Little returned to the dugout alone, with Martinez still on the mound, it was stunning.

Little's reasoning was at least partly understandable. Over the course of the year, the Boston bullpen had proved to be less than trustworthy. Their save percentage ranked below league average and only three other American League teams suffered more relief defeats.

But here was where Little's logic faltered: in the postseason, the bullpen had, out of nowhere, righted itself. In the first 11 playoff games that October, Red Sox relievers had been unscored upon in eight of them and had posted a collective 1.14 ERA while allowing just 16 hits over 31.2 innings.

Little, however, was not about to be swayed by recency bias. When it came to decide between the starter who had been the best pitcher in the game over the previous five seasons or a bunch of relievers who were in the middle of an unexpectedly strong run, that was no decision at all.

His faith would not be rewarded. Jorge Posada roped a double to center, scoring both baserunners and tying the game at 5–5 as Yankee Stadium erupted.

Now Little gave Martinez the hook. *Now* Little went to his bullpen. By then, of course, the damage had been done.

What Little hadn't considered—this was at the dawn of the analytics revolution—was the data that showed that, like most pitching mortals, Martinez had a penchant for wearing down as his pitch count climbed toward triple digits, and by the time Posada connected for a double, Martinez had already thrown 122 pitches.

(Even now, that number is enough to cause you to do a double take. More recently, it's rare for any pitcher to reach 100 pitches in a postseason game, much less one with the pennant at stake. Martinez revealed many years later that Little had told him that he was done after the seventh, only to change his mind before the eighth and ask him to get lefty Nick Johnson out to start the inning. "And I got him out in two pitches," Martinez recalled on TBS. "And then [Little] thought I was going to be better than I was after that. And that's when the wheels fell off.")

The manager had had that information available to him... and chose to disregard it. Right down to his folksy patter, Little was decidedly old-school and had opted to trust his instincts rather than the numbers in front of him.

"Pedro Martinez has been our man all year long and in situations like that, he's the one we want on the mound over anybody we can bring in out of that bullpen," Little would say later.

It was a choice that would cost his team the pennant three innings later, and a few days later, cost Little his job, too.

In the 11th, after Mike Timlin had pitched a perfect ninth and knuckleballer Tim Wakefield retired the Yankees in order in the 10th, Aaron Boone hit the first pitch he saw and drove it into the left field seats.

Game, series, pennant.

With one swing, Boone had handed the Red Sox a setback for the ages, one every bit as bad as 1978 or 1986. But given that this was so sudden, so immediate, it had the power of a gut punch.

There was no build up to this, no rally. One minute, these two teams were battling, in need of extra innings after seven regulation games proved insufficient. And the next minute, Yankee Stadium was thrown into hysteria, with Frank Sinatra's version of "New York, New York" blaring on an endless loop—the whole tableau was the very definition of hell for Red Sox fans.

In a clubhouse quiet enough that you could hear the muffled cries of grown men sobbing, teammate after teammate attempted to console Wakefield and absolve him of the blame. In his office, a subdued Little politely indulged Rudolph Giuliani, who was trying, without much success, to simultaneously revel in his beloved Yankees' triumph and extend comforting words to the losing manager.

"You spend a whole season with these guys, and it hurts," said a subdued Martinez.

It added to the litany of "What if?" questions that dogged the franchise throughout history.

What if journeyman Denny Galehouse had not been chosen for the 1948 playoff game with Cleveland? What if Luis Aparicio had not tripped going around third base in Detroit on the final weekend of the 1972 season, leaving the Red Sox a tantalizing half-game behind the Tigers in a strike-shortened season? What if Lou Piniella had not stuck his glove out to snare Jerry Remy's ninth-inning single in 1978? What if Clemens had not been removed from Game 6 of the 1986 World Series?

This was one more to ponder over the cold New England winters, one more bit of mental anguish to consider.

The Red Sox—and their long-suffering fan base—couldn't have known it that evening of October 16, 2003, but their long nightmare would soon be ending. One year and four nights later, the Red Sox would avenge that loss, and a week after that, they would be crowned champions.

In that sense, the 2003 season closed a chapter of Red Sox history. Over time, it can be regarded as the last time the Sox and their fans had reason to ask: *Why? Why us?*

After the 2004 World Series, every loss that followed would be just...a loss. It wouldn't be one more example of the Baseball Gods inflicting another bit of punishment. It wouldn't be added to the almost endless list of catastrophic losses, another contender for the title of Worst Red Sox Defeat Ever. It wouldn't cause older fans to worry whether they would live to see the day when their team would finally be the last one standing.

The 2003 loss would be the last of its kind. Theologians are free to debate whether it was evidence that God had grown tired of testing the faith of Red Sox fans.

There would be other defeats, of course, as there always are. The Red Sox would get swept out of the playoffs without winning a game in 2005 and come up empty against the Tampa Bay Rays in Game 7 of the 2008 ALCS. They would prove no match for either Cleveland or Houston in 2016 and 2017, respectively, and they would fall short of the pennant in 2021.

But those all came *after.* After the Red Sox shed their history and won it all in 2004, after their fans had finally tasted the ultimate victory, after the crushing losses had been pushed into the corners of their collective memories.

The 2003 loss will never disappear completely. It will resonate some whenever Boone or Wakefield is mentioned, or whenever Little is remembered.

But through the years, its impact has lessened. It's the game you think of when you try to imagine the "before" and "after" picture of Red Sox history.

Redemption was now just around the corner. It would take place in the same ballpark and against the same opponents. And, of course, it would be glorious.

PART 4

THE ICONS

10
Ted Williams

Most athletes have goals, meant to propel them to unimagined heights. Usually, they use them as fuel, to push themselves when the going becomes rough.

Some aim for championships, to experience the ultimate satisfaction of being the last teams standing. Some think in more individual terms, with designs on a particular statistical achievement or All-Star recognition or a personal best performance.

A number of these are never made public, as a means of serving as private motivation.

And then there's Ted Williams.

Williams was, in so many ways, not like anyone else. He wasn't known for his modesty or his lack of belief in himself. He could be brash, or downright cocky, with an ego as big as all outdoors.

So, it should not shock anyone that his goals were different, too. Not for Williams was there any talk of making an All-Star team or winning a batting title.

Those ambitions would have been too pedestrian for Williams, more suitable for mere mortals.

Williams, instead, aimed higher. Much higher.

"All I want out of life is that, when I walk down the street, people will say, 'There goes the greatest hitter who ever lived.'"

Note the "*All* I want" (italics mine), as though he had been hoping for a nice sunrise or a juicy steak.

Williams aimed impossibly high, as high as he could. Damned if he didn't succeed.

It was true a few years into his major league career, when he hit .406, the last time anyone reached the .400 milestone. And it remains true today, more than 60 years after he played his last game, more than 20 years after he passed.

In death, as he was in life, Williams remains the gold standard by which all hitters are measured. From an offensive standpoint, Williams did everything well—except run. Moreover, he did so many things well before they were even considered important parts of a player's profile.

It wasn't until the early 2000s that much value was placed on on-base percentage, but long before it became exploited as a market inefficiency in Moneyball, Williams finished with a career OBP of .482. Decades and decades before people got around to understanding the value of a walk, Williams, ever ahead of his time, averaged nearly a walk per game.

Launch angles? They became all the rage in the second decade of the 21st century, as if everyone conveniently forgot that Williams swung with a natural loft to his swing, driving pitches over the heads of infielders and, often, over walls, too.

And it shouldn't surprise you to learn that, long before infield shifts became commonplace, Williams inspired the first ones, so desperate were opposing teams to keep him off base.

In other words, before we had a way to measure a hitter's excellence, Williams was already demonstrating what it was like to be the best of the best. While others were satisfied with a "grip it and rip it" approach, Williams was turning hitting into an art form. Hell, he wrote a book on the subject and presciently called it *The Science of Hitting.*

The amazing thing, really, is that Williams may have undersold his ambition.

Beyond being, inarguably, the greatest hitter who ever lived, Williams was so much more. When he wasn't on the baseball field, excelling where mere mortals failed, Williams was establishing himself as the standard-bearer in other areas.

He was an expert fly fisherman and deep-sea fisherman, elected to the International Game Fish Association Hall of Fame.

In World War II and again in the Korean War, Williams proved himself an expert fighter pilot, serving as a flight instructor in World War II before flying 39 combat missions for the Marine Corps, earning two gold medals. No less an authority than former astronaut John Glenn, his Korean War wingman, called Williams one of the best pilots he had ever known.

It was as though Williams had grown bored becoming baseball's best hitter and sought new horizons, new fields to conquer.

(It should be noted that Williams did not exactly go willingly into service. After first attempting to reclassify his draft status due to being his mother's only viable means of financial support, Williams somewhat reluctantly enlisted. And he bristled that he was chosen from the inactive reserves to see combat in Korea. But he twice passed up opportunities to serve his hitch as a member of the armed services baseball team.)

In so many ways, Williams came to represent the 20th century American male archetype. Tall and handsome, accomplished at everything he tried, he was almost mythic in his achievement.

Though flawed in his personal life—he was married three times and, by his own admission, often an absent, inattentive father—his public persona was unmatched.

Williams was the embodiment of an All-American. And for the entirety of his playing career, he belonged only to the Red Sox.

From the beginning, as a 20-year-old rookie, Williams proved to be something special. Just past his teenage years, he led the American League in RBI and total bases and, in a precursor of seasons to come, intentional walks, too.

Even in his first year, no one wanted to pitch to Williams if they didn't have to. Ballplayers must earn their reputations, and that is something that can take years. But Williams had gotten the attention—and the respect—of pitchers and managers right from the start.

Throughout his career, Williams sometimes had adequate protection in the rest of the Red Sox lineup, though sometimes he did not. Whether he was surrounded by Jimmie Foxx or Joe Cronin or Bobby Doerr, or, as was sometimes the case, run-of-the-mill major leaguers, Williams still dominated.

His hitting philosophy, for all its intricacies—Williams also highlighted "heat maps" decades before the practice was commonplace—was sometimes remarkably simple.

"Get a good pitch," Williams would counsel, "and hit it."

That would be akin to Picasso advising aspiring painters: "Pick out a color you like and work with it." Easier said than done.

When Williams had the benefit of Foxx or Doerr hitting either ahead of him or behind him, he was more likely to get better pitches. But his approach didn't change much depending on his supporting cast.

For Williams, the act of hitting was like a game of cat-and-mouse. Just as the best hitters can't connect on every swing, Williams understood that even the best pitchers couldn't be expected to locate every pitch with precision. When the pitcher failed to keep the ball out of the middle of the plate, *that* was the time for the hitter to pounce.

In essence, Williams saw each at-bat as an exercise in probability, the same way an expert card shark might regard each new hand. With every pitch thrown, the circumstances changed and so did the odds. It was Williams' job to assess how to best mitigate against all the independent factors—the pitcher, the score, the count, the umpire—and capitalize on the best opportunity.

It is likely that no major leaguer ever spent more time thinking about hitting. While stationed in left field, Williams was known to take practice swings in between pitches, like an overeager Little Leaguer counting the minutes until his next turn at bat.

When he wasn't swinging or thinking about hitting, Williams loved to talk hitting. He frequently sought out the game's best—he became friendly with both Ty Cobb and Rogers Hornsby—and would listen to their philosophies and contrast them to his own.

The notion of Williams seeking out former greats to tap into their hitting expertise would come full-circle in Teddy Ballgame's later years.

He was less enamored with baserunning or playing defense. To Williams, those were mere interruptions to what he wished to do most. (Had the DH existed in Williams' day, he doubtless would have campaigned to fill that role, discarding the other aspects of the game as mere nuisances. And it's scary indeed to think what he might have been able to do with the benefit of video. Imagine the game's greatest hitter having the ability to break down his at-bats in super slow motion, evaluated in real time?)

Even now, his numbers seem cartoonishly inflated. Many baseball historians regard his 1941 season, when he was all of 22, as perhaps the best ever for a hitter. That season, Williams led the major leagues in homers (37), runs scored (135), on-base percentage (.553), slugging percentage (.735), and intentional walks.

His OPS+—which aims to measure a player's ability to get on base and hit for extra bases, measured against the rest of the league, and adjusted for the player's home ballpark—was 235+, meaning he was 135 percent better than the league average for that year.

And, of course, using more traditional statistical measures, he hit .406 that season, a feat not since duplicated.

Two players came close in the span of four years. In 1977, Rod Carew hit .388 and in 1980, Kansas City's George Brett hit .390. Both times, their pursuit of the elusive .400 milestone made national news; both times, they came up short. Neither, it should be noted, came close to matching Williams' all-around excellence at the plate. Carew managed just 14 homers that year and, for the only time in his Hall of Fame career, knocked in 100 runs. Meanwhile, Brett benefited from playing only 117 games.

Baseball's analytic revolution in the 21st century devalued the notion of batting average. For most, on-base percentage and slugging percentage came to serve as the best measuring sticks of a hitter. Where once winning a batting title was the ultimate achievement for a hitter, now it's outmoded.

Still, there's something to be said for a statistical achievement that has gone unmatched for more than 80 years and counting.

If there's a blemish to the career of Ted Williams, it's that, for all his brilliance as a hitter, he never realized a championship. Only twice, in fact, did Williams come close. In 1946, the Red Sox won their first and only American League pennant of his career, before failing to the St. Louis Cardinals in seven games in the World Series.

Two years later, the Red Sox finished the regular season tied with Cleveland, then lost a one-game playoff game for the pennant.

That was it. Nineteen seasons, and one trip to the World Series.

How much of that was Williams' fault? Little, it would seem. For too many years, Red Sox management ignored the importance of pitching, and it surely didn't help that, over the second half of his career, the Red Sox stubbornly refused to integrate.

Still, the lack of a title on his résumé is frequently cited when Williams' career is matched with Joe DiMaggio and Stan Musial, his two most worthy contemporaries.

But was it his fault that the Red Sox failed to surround him with a better supporting cast? Can he be blamed that the Sox foolishly and ignorantly failed to take advantage of the sudden availability of Black players?

Williams owns another historical distinction, too, as perhaps the first modern player to openly duel with the media.

Often, he found their questions to be needlessly confrontational and their assumptions about him ill-founded.

His antipathy toward Boston reporters was not without merit. Some appeared to punish his lack of cooperation by leaving him off postseason award ballots, and often, those snubs—personal vendettas, really—cost Williams dearly when it came to Most Valuable Player award voting.

Williams twice was voted American League MVP, but on four other occasions finished second, including, incredibly, his 1941 Triple Crown season.

Over the years, *Boston Record* columnist Dave Egan referred to Williams as, among other things, "the prize heel ever to wear a Boston uniform," "the most overpaid buffoon in the history of baseball," and "the inventor of the automatic choke."

In balloting for the AL MVP in 1941, Egan was said to have left Williams off his ballot altogether when even a down-ballot vote would have been enough to lift Williams ahead of DiMaggio, the winner that year.

One shudders to think what Williams would do in the age of talk radio. But in the 1980s, as a young producer for a talk show in Providence, Rhode Island, I got something of a hint.

It was my job to book guests for a nightly two-hour sport talk show, *Chuck Wilson on Sports*, on WEAN, a news-talk station. Together, Chuck and I had befriended the gentleman who was in charge of Williams' hitting camp in Lakeville, Massachusetts, a fan and regular listener of the show.

On a whim, we had mentioned that having Ted on the show—via telephone—would be the ultimate dream guest. The director said he would do his best to see if he could one day arrange it. Neither Wilson nor I gave it a second thought.

But late one afternoon several months later, the phone rang in our office. Much to our delight and utter shock, we were told that Williams had agreed to come on that evening. We were given a phone number to call at a prescribed time and assured that Williams would join us.

That night, as I joined Wilson on the air as a co-host, Williams was an utterly charming guest, taking calls from awe-struck listeners, answering questions in detail, and genuinely enjoying himself.

We were astonished at our good fortune. As we neared the top of the hour—Williams had been a guest for about 40 minutes—Wilson began wrapping up the interview, thanking Williams for his time and generosity when he was quickly interrupted.

"Chuck, Sean....you two guys are two of the biggest con artists I've ever met," said Williams, with a gleeful chuckle punctuating his familiar booming voice. "You told me I was gonna come on for 15 minutes, and you kept me for almost three-quarters of an hour. But that's OK, I enjoyed it. Bye."

Click, the line went dead.

Wilson and I stared at each other, our mouths agape, for what seemed like a minute, filling the program with dead air. We had, in fact, never even talked about how long the segment would last and figured we would keep Williams as long as he would allow. We had made no mention of "15 minutes," or any other designated time limit.

Wilson recovered in time to go to a commercial break, at which point we burst into a nervous laughter. Had that really just happened? Had we really just been (unfairly) called out by The Kid? By then, it was irrelevant. We had just finished 45 minutes with the Greatest Hitter Who Ever Lived, and nothing else mattered.

In his later years, Williams, known to be cantankerous at times, seemed to make peace with the idolatry that existed around him. At the insistence of his son, Williams capitalized on his name and earned a small fortune signing autographs—something he was often loath to do as a player. He made public appearances and appeared more comfortable, both with his own celebrity and in his own skin.

When the Red Sox hosted the 1999 MLB All-Star Game at Fenway for the first time since 1961—the year after Williams' retirement—Williams was the crown jewel of the event.

At the time, the Home Run Derby was just beginning to become a signature event and with such sluggers as Mark McGwire and Sammy Sosa in attendance, the derby was indeed one of the highlights of the proceedings.

But the real climax came just before the game itself. With the baselines stacked with the game's top stars, Williams was driven to the mound in an old bullpen cart, waving his hat in recognition of the wild applause he received.

With the cart parked atop the pitcher's mound, the biggest names in the game approached him the way children might approach Santa Claus—with genuine awe and a little trepidation. Tony Gwynn, like Williams a San Diego native, leaned in to talk hitting with the master. McGwire and others somewhat meekly offered their thoughts, grateful for their audience.

Around the ballpark, a steady roar from fans was maintained. They were watching the franchise's biggest star, soon to be 81 and in failing health, make one more pilgrimage to the ballpark where he made his debut 60 years prior. As a bonus, they watched as present-day superstars did all but genuflect at his side.

It was like watching a sequel to *Field of Dreams*. Had they cancelled the game that was to begin minutes later, not a single fan would have complained. The night had already been made magic.

Then, as if the Red Sea had parted, the players dispersed, and the bullpen cart, driven by longtime Fenway Park employee Al Forester, whose tenure with the club dated back to the last few seasons of Williams' playing career, began to pull away.

As his protégé, Carl Yastrzemski, had done on foot 16 years earlier, Williams was taking a victory lap, once more wildly waving his cap in response to the din.

The players assumed their positions and watched as Williams was ferried out to center field, where he was driven through the giant garage door under the bleachers. Some of the players waved, too, now appearing as small as Little Leaguers by comparison.

The 60 or so players representing both leagues, the best baseball had to offer, and the sold-out crowd had been given a treat they would never forget. With the air thick with emotion and more than a little disbelief, a few—in the stands and on the field—undoubtedly pointed as Williams was driven off to center and noted to someone nearby, "There goes the greatest hitter who ever lived."

11

Carl Yastrzemski

It would be difficult to imagine a professional athlete who was in a more unenviable position than Carl Yastrzemski in 1961.

Yastrzemski was breaking into the big leagues as the Boston Red Sox's new left fielder, which would be challenging enough. Yastrzemski was tasked with making the leap from Triple A to Boston and all the expectations that came with such a jump: better competition, tougher pitching, a longer schedule with more travel, and the scrutiny that came with being in the majors for the first time.

That would be plenty for any young player.

But for Yastrzemski, that was just the beginning. He had all of that with which to contend, and the impossible expectations that came with replacing only the Greatest Hitter Who Ever Lived.

Ted Williams, who was not shy about embracing that title, had retired the previous September, having accumulated a lifetime batting average of .344, won six batting titles (including his final one at age 38), belted 521 home runs, and earned two Most Valuable Player awards and five other finishes in the top three of MVP voting, as well as 17 All-Star selections.

Williams would later write a book titled *The Science of Hitting,* and it would seem not at all boastful or overstated. Had he not missed three full seasons and large parts of two others, there's little doubt he would have neared 700 career homers and amassed well over 3,000 hits.

Williams didn't merely cast a shadow when he retired; he damn near blotted out the sun. Having established himself as the best hitter to ever play the game—a title that remains more than six decades after his retirement and some 20 years after his passing—he set an impossible standard to match.

Over the course of his first six seasons, Yastrzemski struggled to establish his own identity. He was not without his accomplishments. He won the American League batting title in 1963 and also led the league in doubles that season. He won two Gold Gloves for his defensive play in left and was chosen for the All-Star team three times.

In five of his first six seasons, he posted an OPS of .799 or better. But as even his biggest supporters would acknowledge, he was not making anyone forget Williams. Never mind that such an ask would have been impossible.

Beyond the impossible standards he was expected to meet or surpass, Yastrzemski couldn't have been any different from Williams when it came to personality.

While Williams carried himself with supreme confidence, his voice booming and his authority in the batter's box unchallenged, Yastrzemski was smaller in both stature and presence. While Williams was towering at 6'3", Yaz stood under 6'0".

And while Williams could immediately dominate a room—or a clubhouse or dugout—with his commanding aura, Yastrzemski was far more circumspect, content to blend in, or preferably, escape altogether.

Fairly or not, Williams made hitting look easy or, at least, appear to be the most natural activity imaginable. For Yastrzemski, hitting was hard work. It required hours in the batting cage, constant adjustments, and interminable experimentation. The discipline to become the hitter he became took a lot out of him. In today's ballplayer parlance, Yastrzemski succeeded because of a willingness to "grind."

Intuitively, he seemed to understand this and recognize that, in comparison to others, he was little more than a dedicated blue-collar worker. Once, noting the pride he took in reaching both the 3,000-hit and 400-homer zenith, he noted that other more famous hitters—like Williams, Joe DiMaggio, or Lou Gehrig—failed to achieve one or the other.

"They were Cadillacs," noted Yaz, "and I'm a Chevrolet."

At the plate, Williams could make the bat appear to be a mere extension of his own body, an appendage to enable him to do what he was born to do: hit a baseball. By contrast, Yastrzemski's bat was more of a tool from his workbag, in the way a wrench would be for a plumber or a hammer for a carpenter.

Williams was the brilliant if temperamental artist at whom others would marvel as he sought perfection; Yastrzemski was the guy on the assembly line, hands callused, brow sweaty, dedicating himself to finishing the job.

As different as they were in appearance and countenance, the two were linked in one significant way: by their teams' irrelevance.

In a career that spanned parts of four decades, Williams reached the postseason exactly once, winning the American League pennant in 1946. The rest of the time, the Sox were often an afterthought in the American League standings.

At times, Williams hardly seemed bothered by his team's failure to compete. Wasn't he the game's best hitter? Wasn't he the standard by which all other hitters were measured? Weren't his four plate appearances each day—hitting clinics, conducted by the master himself—enough?

In terms of team performance, Yastrzemski's first six seasons were exercises in futility. In that span, the team never came close to posting a winning record or finished closer than 19 games out of first. In 1965, when Yastrzemski enjoyed his best season to date (.312/.395/.536 with a career-high 20 homers and a league-leading 45 doubles), the Red Sox lost 100 games and finished next-to-last in the 10-team league.

And while Williams got a pass on the matter of team success, Yastrzemski was tagged as the chief culprit. He was the team's best player, in his prime. Why hadn't he made the Sox better? Why hadn't he willed them to a pennant?

So, in 1967, he did just that. And "willed" wasn't much of an exaggeration. Tired of losing and believing that he could elevate his own game with enough effort, Yastrzemski dedicated himself to a demanding off-season workout program—the kind that, today, would be unremarkable for a pro athlete, but at the time was virtually unprecedented.

He spent the winter between the 1966 and 1967 seasons at an area hotel gym, lifting weights and generally punishing his body, dedicating himself to have his best season. He was 28 and six straight losing seasons had served to, at once, demoralize him and motivate him.

The result was a season for the ages. Yastrzemski, under a new taskmaster in Dick Williams, had one of the greatest seasons in modern baseball history, capturing the Triple Crown—a feat that wouldn't be matched for more than 40 years.

Just how dominant was Yastrzemski's season? As measured by WAR (Wins Above Replacement), Yastrzemski compiled a 12.4. To put that into perspective, no Red Sox position player has topped that. Williams' best season was 10.7, a figure matched in 2018 by Mookie Betts.

In fact, in the modern era (1900–present), only five players have posted a single-season WAR total greater than Yastrzemski's that season: Babe Ruth, Walter Johnson, Pete Alexander, Steve Carlton, and Dwight Gooden. Of those, only Ruth was a position player.

There were other quality players who were part of the Impossible Dream Red Sox in 1967. Jim Lonborg, who had pitched two unremarkable seasons prior to '67, won 22 games, logged 277.1 innings, and captured the Cy Young Award. Shortstop Rico Petrocelli and first baseman George Scott contributed strong seasons, too.

But the 1967 Red Sox were, first and foremost, Yaz's team. His batting stance, with the bat held impossibly high and straight, became the one for kids throughout New England—especially those who hit lefthanded—to emulate.

Soon, he was seen on TV endorsing products—everything from bread to mustard to cars.

On the final weekend of the season, he went 6-for-8 in the final two games, pushing the Sox over the finish line to their first pennant in 21 seasons. He was nearly as brilliant in the World Series with 10 hits—three of them home runs—and five RBI. But it wasn't enough to beat Bob Gibson and the St. Louis Cardinals.

Sadly, that fall would represent a microcosm of Yastrzemski's career. He would enjoy individual success—though he would never again match the stunning numbers from 1967—but fall short of realizing the ultimate goal of winning a championship.

At times, he would come frustratingly close. In 1975, his team would again take the best National League champions of that decade to a seventh game of the World Series and again lose. Three years later, matched against the archrival Yankees in a one-game playoff to claim the American League East title, the Sox again came up short.

For a chunk of his 23 seasons with the Red Sox—and especially between the 1967 and 1975 pennant-winning seasons—Yastrzemski became the focal point of fans' frustration. Sometimes, this had to do with his habit of not always running hard to first on routine groundouts, but mostly it stemmed from his identity as the face of the franchise.

Having willed an otherwise underwhelming roster to the brink of a title in 1967, frustrated Red Sox fans began to hold Yastrzemski responsible for the team's collective shortcomings. When the Sox fell short by a half-game in the 1972 AL East race, Yastrzemski became the scapegoat. The same was true two seasons later when the Sox collapsed like a folding chair in the final five weeks, going from division leaders to a third-place finish.

It was his great misfortune that he made the final out of the 1978 playoff game and the final out of Game 7 of the 1975 World Series. The inability to rescue his team from defeat in two season-ending losses no doubt gnawed at Yastrzemski, ever the perfectionist. But it also enabled some to permanently link him to his team's failures.

Once again, Yastrzemski became the target of their ire.

It didn't help that the perception persisted that Yastrzemski was a favorite of longtime owner Thomas A Yawkey. Yawkey, who was childless, adopted an almost paternal relationship with his star players. He paid them handsomely, even before the days of free agency and salary arbitration, and fairly or not, Yastrzemski came to be seen as the owner's pet, beyond reproach.

As Yastrzemski aged, his profile began to recede some, especially after 1978. The Red Sox had, over the previous handful of seasons, developed a new generation of homegrown stars from Carlton Fisk to Jim Rice and Fred Lynn. They, rather than Yaz, were now the linchpins, the fresh faces of the franchise.

Still, Yastrzemski soldiered on, converting from outfielder to first baseman, and occasionally, in recognition of his age, DH. The Red Sox were no longer his team, which afforded him a sort of elder statesman status.

In his remaining years, he evolved, transitioning from superstar to legend emeritus. Instead of demanding he deliver the elusive World Series win to them, fans cheered his pursuit of personal milestones—3,000 career hits and 400 career homers.

By 1983, before which Yastrzemski announced his plans to retire, he had achieved living legend status, the connective tissue back to another era, pre-expansion.

When Yastrzemski began his major league career, the American League didn't have a team west of Kansas City; now it had three. When he debuted, teams occasionally traveled by train; now, they were flown in chartered jets. The designated hitter, double-knit uniforms, expanded playoffs, divisional formats, 162-game schedules, free agency, and myriad other innovations, good and bad, were all introduced after his major league career began.

The 1983 season became a year-long salute to Yaz, with each city offering retirement gifts and pregame ceremonies. Still not comfortable in the spotlight, nearly a quarter century after he first entered it, Yastrzemski mostly endured the attention and gestures of goodwill, but he was too private, too reserved, too damn self-conscious to actually enjoy all of it.

It became one more thing—like questions from reporters, affection from fans, and unrealistic expectations—that he merely abided.

But on the final week of the 1983 season—one that, fittingly, ended with the Sox as nonfactors in the pennant race, something about Yastrzemski seemed to soften.

It was as if Yastrzemski came to recognize that this was his chance to drop the façade and allow fans to see the real Yaz at last.

After all the testimonials and speeches were made and the gifts presented, it was time for the final, long goodbye.

Then, to the surprise of just about everyone present, Yastrzemski embarked on a personal victory lap around Fenway, jogging along the warning track circling the field and slapping the outstretched hands of the fans who longed for a connection.

Stoic, reserved, intensely private Yaz was literally pressing the flesh, the way a politician might on a campaign stop, turning the old ballpark into one giant rope line farewell.

(A dozen years later, Cal Ripken Jr., on the night in which he broke Lou Gehrig's record for most consecutive games played, employed the same strategy as he circled Camden Yards in Baltimore. At the time, few if any noted that Yastrzemski had initiated the idea.)

Since his retirement, Yastrzemski has faded even deeper into anonymity. When the Red Sox need his prized autograph on a box of baseballs for a special event or for charity, an employee delivers them to a well-known butcher shop where the legend is known to regularly spend time, chatting with longtime friends in the privacy of a back storage room. The following day, the employee returns for the signed balls.

On the rare occasions when the Red Sox request his presence at Fenway—throwing out the first pitch of a World Series game, for instance—Yastrzemski reluctantly cooperates.

When he enters the field from the dugout to a rapturous greeting, he typically holds his hand way above his head in a sort of perfunctory wave—a gesture that seems half acknowledgment and half "please, stop"—all the while staring at the ground.

There is no documentation that he has left his car idling outside on Van Ness St., the better to facilitate a quicker getaway from the ballpark, but such a disclosure would surprise few.

In truth, Yaz was never comfortable in the spotlight, preferring to blend into the background and keep to himself. He tended to befriend players who shared his interest in fishing and other solitary pursuits. Had he played in the era of social media, it's likely he would have found that to be suffocating.

Even the arrival to the big leagues of his own grandson, San Francisco Giants outfielder Mike Yastrzemski, has failed to bring the elder Yastrzemski out his self-imposed shell. After being cajoled by his daughter, Mike's mother, to fly to San Francisco to see his grandson make his debut in 2019, he's now content to watch Mike's games on TV—as long as, he noted, they don't conclude too late from the West Coast.

There's an inescapable irony to Yastrzemski's late-in-life reserve. So often compared to Williams, the man he was doomed to replace in 1961, Yastrzemski has, decades later, become even more private than Williams was thought to be.

In actuality, Williams nearly became a public presence in his dotage, before his health deteriorated, as if forgetting why it was so important for him to maintain his privacy all those years. Williams, whose ego was considerable, luxuriated in his status as the Greatest Hitter Who Ever Lived and determined that forgoing his privacy was a worthwhile sacrifice in exchange for the hosanas that greeted him wherever he went.

Yastrzemski, of course, had no such appellation due him. But he retired with more games played, more hits collected, and more seasons completed than Williams. And today, whether it makes a difference to him or not, he has the honor of being the greatest living Red Sox player.

12
David Ortiz

For decades, the biggest Red Sox stars, the players who came to define the franchise, all finished their careers short one highly important achievement.

They had gaudy statistics, had won numerous awards, and were celebrated for their careers. Each won a permanent place in the hearts of generations of Red Sox fans.

But each of them, from Ted Williams to Carl Yastrzemski—Hall of Famers both—failed to win a championship.

They could list their accomplishments—the batting titles, the Gold Gloves, even the Triple Crowns—but in the end, a recap of their time with the Red Sox would have the same, sad ending—a familiar, qualifying reminder of a career that fell short by one important measurement.

"...But he never won a World Series."

For decades, it seemed like it was part of some Faustian bargain. Yes, you will be adored throughout New England. Yes, legions of fans will offer their remembrances of you to their children and grandchildren. Yes, you will be immortalized in Cooperstown with the rest of the game's all-time greats.

But no, sadly, you will not realize the ultimate baseball experience. You will not celebrate with your teammates in the final game of the season. You will, instead, have your career end with one box left unchecked.

And like too many others in franchise history, that, too, will be part of your legacy.

In the pre-expansion era, with no division, no League Championship Series, and certainly, no wild cards, Williams appeared in just one World Series over a career that stretched across four decades.

Yastrzemski got two cracks at the Fall Classic, each ending the same way: in defeat, in Game 7.

But for David Ortiz, fate had other ideas. He won his first World Series—and the team's first in 86 years—in his second season in Boston. He got another three years later, and still another six years after the second.

When he retired after the 2016 season, he was the lone player to have been part of the franchise's three most recent championships, the common thread that connected championships nine years apart.

The three World Series do not begin to compare to the 10 won by Yogi Berra, or, crossing sports, the 11 championships won by Bill Russell of the Celtics. Then again, those players were part of dynastic teams that dominated in an era featuring far fewer teams.

Still, winning three World Series with one franchise is no small feat. In fact, for players who never played for the Yankees, it's been accomplished by just a handful of others.

Such a lofty distinction probably felt impossibly beyond his grasp in December 2002, for the out-of-work Ortiz.

Weeks earlier, the Minnesota Twins had, after much internal debate, opted to non-tender Ortiz, making him a free agent.

The combination of a small-market team, ever-mindful of its payroll limitations, and a rather unremarkable six seasons in Minneapolis yielded this regrettable call. The Twins, managed at the time by Tom Kelly, had tried, without success, to mold Ortiz into something he was most assuredly not: a contact hitter who valued putting the ball in play above all else.

That was not Ortiz's strength, nor would it ever be his identity. Ortiz was a big, strong run producer, but one who ran hot-and-cold, and was liable to strike out a lot. In Kelly's mind, this made Ortiz an offensive liability.

The prospect of going to salary arbitration and paying Ortiz for the promise of more consistent production proved too risky for the Twins. Minnesota's general manager, Terry Ryan, an honest and accountable executive, would take full blame in the years to come for the organization's blunder.

It's worth noting, however, that when the Twins set Ortiz free, what followed was not exactly a stampede for his services.

To the contrary, it took a phone call from Pedro Martinez in the Dominican Republic to help call attention to Ortiz's availability and his possible fit for the Red Sox's roster.

Ortiz's career began modestly enough. For a time in 2003, he found himself in a job-share arrangement with the ignominious Jeremy Giambi. Not until May, by which time Ortiz had contemplated requesting his release from the Red Sox because of irregular playing time, was he an everyday lineup fixture.

Ortiz's slow ascent to stardom offered no indication he would someday be regarded as one of the Red Sox's all-time greats. But given the opportunity as an everyday player for the first time in his career, Ortiz hit 31 homers and knocked in 101, and he did it in just 128 games.

That postseason, however, he gave no indication that he would soon come to be recognized as one of the game's most clutch October performers. In 10 games—a five-game ALDS against Oakland, followed by the epic seven-game ALCS showdown with the Yankees—Ortiz homered twice, but hit just .191.

It would take another year for Ortiz to become the fully formed slugger with a flair for the dramatic on the game's biggest stage.

It helped greatly that Ortiz was surrounded by a far more formidable surrounding cast than he had ever experienced in Minnesota. Certainly, there was no Manny Ramirez hitting ahead of or behind him with the Twins.

The ballpark played a role, as well. The Metrodome had artificial turf and was perfect for speedy, athletic players. In Fenway, meanwhile, Ortiz found the perfect environment. While hitting the ball out to straightaway right field required a prodigious poke, the inviting left field wall was the perfect target for doubles when Ortiz took pitches the other way with an inside-out swing.

Coming to Boston freed Ortiz as a hitter and a teammate. While the Twins tried to change who he was as a hitter, Ortiz could be more himself with the Sox—both in the batter's box and in the clubhouse. The environment was looser, and he could express his outsize personality.

"I felt like I just got out of jail, bro," Ortiz wrote in his autobiography, *Big Papi*. "I felt like I could just hit the way I wanted to hit."

* * *

It's not as if the Red Sox had never had a clutch superstar before. After all, though he made the final out in both the 1975 World Series and the one-game playoff with the Yankees in 1978, Yastrzemski had some of his best performances when his team needed him most—on the final weekend of the 1967 season and in the World Series versus the Cardinals that followed.

That Yastrzemski's teams never won it all was hardly The Captain's fault. Sometimes, perception and reality don't dovetail.

But there can be little doubt of Ortiz's penchant for the big hits in the biggest games, or his embrace of the Big Moment. While some shrink in the face of such a challenge, ruled by fear of failure, others see an opportunity. Chalk it up to determination, ego, or what-have-you, Ortiz was one such player.

"I guess it was just the ability to focus," said Ortiz in 2018. "Sometimes, you have to have that, where you don't get distracted by the pressure, from the noise or whatever or the tension."

Ironically, Ortiz's ascension as one of the game's most feared clutch hitters came at a time when the arrival of analytics began to question whether such a characterization could exist. With a more careful, data-based study of the game, analysts maintained that an examination of postseason games and the occasional regular season "big game" constituted too small a sample size to make a determination.

Performing well in a handful of games that happened to take place in October did not, these analysts maintained, constitute an ability to come through in the clutch; rather, the sample size was too small to result in any meaningful conclusions.

Clutch, in other words, was a myth.

A generation of Red Sox fans would beg to differ.

If Ortiz's origin story as Mr. Clutch had a starting point, it was Game 4 of the 2004 American League Championship. The Red Sox had lost the first three games of the series, including a lopsided 19–8 defeat in Game 3 that served to presage an embarrassing sweep that seemed destined to conclude in Game 4 at Fenway.

But after the Red Sox improbably rallied to tie the game in the bottom of the ninth, it took Ortiz's home run heroics in the 12th inning before the Sox could claim victory. Having already homered in the bottom of the 10th to win Game 3 of the ALDS against the Anaheim Angels, Ortiz became the first player in baseball history to hit two walk-off homers in the same postseason.

The next night, he again played the role of hero, sending the Sox (and the series) back to New York, where the Sox won twice more and finished off the Yankees.

The 2004 postseason heroics were only a preview of coming attractions when it came to Ortiz supplying the big hit in the biggest moments.

From his first season in Boston (2003) through 2006, Ortiz registered 15 walk-off hits during the regular season. But naturally, it was the postseason where Ortiz shone brightest.

In 2007, he hit .714 in a first-round sweep of the Angels, and in the World Series triumph over Colorado, knocked in four runs in four games.

The 2013 postseason, however, put Ortiz in a whole other category when it came to providing dramatic moments with the bat.

In the ALCS, with the Sox having dropped the opener against Detroit, the Sox were seemingly headed for another defeat in Game 2, trailing by four in the bottom of the eighth. But Ortiz cranked a game-tying grand slam into the Boston bullpen—taking Tigers outfielder Torii Hunter, in futile pursuit of the ball, with it.

The series shifted with that shot, with the Sox winning in the bottom of the ninth, then taking three of the next four to capture the pennant.

It was the 2013 World Series where Ortiz made his most lasting October imprint. Cardinals manager Mike Matheny stubbornly ordered his pitchers to continue pitching to Ortiz, even with an open base available. Was Matheny unaware of Ortiz's accomplishments on the big stage? Did he think he had uncovered some secret plan that had somehow escaped every other MLB manager of the last decade or so?

That World Series, Ortiz hit .688 with an on-base percentage of .760 and a slugging percentage of 1.188. Naturally, he was the obvious choice as MVP.

* * *

What's remarkable about these three Red Sox icons is that each one of them played into his forties, a rare display of longevity in any era.

Owing no small amount to his ability to focus solely on hitting as a designated hitter, Ortiz was able to plow forward into his forties and remain productive. As a DH, Ortiz could reduce the wear-and-tear on his body by about half. Instead of lumbering around the first base bag and risking the muscle pulls and strains that come with playing defense, Ortiz could save his body and spend time reviewing video of his previous at-bats.

In 2016, his final season with the Red Sox, Ortiz performed like a slugger half his age. He led the American League in RBI while leading all of baseball in doubles, slugging percentage, and OPS. In fact, only three times over his career had he posted a higher OPS than the 1.021 he had in his last season.

As Ortiz dominated at 40, pressure built throughout his final season to continue playing in 2017 and beyond. The Red Sox would have certainly welcomed him back and money would not have been an object.

But even to perform only as a DH, Ortiz had beaten his body up. Few knew of the physical pounding he absorbed in the later years of his career, or what he needed to do just to prepare for games: the massages, the treatment for his aching feet and heels.

Ortiz decided that he had enough. Like Yastrzemski, Ortiz got the hero treatment when visiting every road city for the final time, bestowed with gifts and well wishes.

The Red Sox qualified for the postseason in his final year, winning the division and headed for a division series showdown with Cleveland. But the Sox were a flawed bunch, thin on pitching, and were ignominiously swept.

After the game, Ortiz emerged from the home dugout and walked solemnly to the mound, where, with tears in his eyes, he waved goodbye to the fans who had stayed through the final out.

There was resignation in his eyes, some of it no doubt occasioned by his team's dismal showing in the postseason, and perhaps more than a little regret that he hadn't done more (1-for-9 with one RBI in three games) in his final opportunity.

This was not, after all, how the greatest clutch hitter in team history was supposed to go out. He hadn't homered in his final at-bat, as Williams famously did. And while Yastrzemski's final goodbye was part of a weekend-long tribute, with the fate of the 1983 Red Sox long ago decided, there was a suddenness to Ortiz's valedictory salute.

For 20 seasons, Ortiz had specialized in the Big Moment. In a perfect world, the 2016 Red Sox would have overcome their deficiencies, motivated to send Ortiz out as a winner one last time. But this final chapter would have no perfect ending.

Still, the disappointment was temporary. In short order, Ortiz could look back on a career that would see him finish second to Williams in homers, third in RBI behind Yastrzemski and Williams.

But, of course, he could claim something neither of the others could: championships. Three, in fact.

With some luck, he might have added two more in 2003 and 2008. Then again, Ortiz had been plenty fortunate already. Rescued from the scrap heap, on his third team, Ortiz achieved a legacy no one in team history could match. On a team so often defined by close calls, near misses, and devastating defeat, Ortiz was the ultimate winner.

PART 5

THE ACES

13

Roger Clemens

IN THEIR LONG HISTORY, THE RED SOX NEVER HAD A SHORTAGE of dynamic stars.

They had Babe Ruth, only the greatest player ever, and Ted Williams, the greatest hitter the game ever knew.

They had, at one time or another, Jimmie Foxx, Tris Speaker, Bobby Doerr, and Joe Cronin.

They had the last .400 hitter (Williams), the last American Leaguer with 400 or more total bases (Jim Rice), and the game's last Triple Crown winner for a stretch of 45 seasons (Carl Yastrzemski).

They had the youngest player to ever lead the league in homers (Tony Conigliaro), and a lengthy list of batting title winners.

They've had their own Hall of Famers, and briefly, others who made pit stops in Boston at the end of their careers

(Orlando Cepeda, Luis Aparicio, Rickey Henderson, Andre Dawson).

What they didn't have, for the longest time, was an honest-to-goodness, homegrown ace.

In the 1960s, Jim Lonborg hinted at becoming one before a skiing accident after the magical 1967 season interceded. Still, Lonborg did win a Cy Young Award.

To that end, the Sox once had Cy Young himself, though not, it should be noted, until he had already enjoyed the prime of his career elsewhere.

There were the occasional exceptions. Mel Parnell, later a team broadcaster, might have referred to himself as "a fine young man with a fine young arm" when the lefty averaged better than 18 wins per season from the late 1940s through the mid-1950s, but his career lasted just 10 years.

Mostly, the Red Sox were an offense-first franchise, always capable of scoring runs by the bushelful, but at times equally capable of giving up at least as many as they scored, if not more.

In retrospect—just spitballing here—it's possible the team's inattentiveness to the pitching part of the game may have contributed at least somewhat to their 86 seasons without a championship.

But in the 1980s, that changed.

In the 1983 draft, the Red Sox used their first-round selection, the 19th pick overall, to choose Roger Clemens from the University of Texas. In less than a year, he made his major league debut; within three years, he had become arguably the best starting pitcher in the American League.

Clemens was straight out of central casting: a big, strapping, fireballing righthander, a Texas gunslinger on the mound. He was strong and powerful. And best of all for the Red Sox, he was all theirs. (Clemens was actually chosen out of high school by the New York Mets but chose to attend Texas. The mere thought of the Mets having the tandem of Clemens and Dwight Gooden in the same rotation in the 1980s is mind-boggling.)

It didn't take long for Clemens to graduate to the big leagues. He made all of 18 appearances in the minors, and even that brief apprenticeship, in retrospect, may have been unnecessary. Teams were usually reluctant to rush their best pitching prospects to the big leagues, out of fear that they would be missing valuable development time.

Clemens was nearly fully formed when the Sox chose him. He was an All-America selection in both years at Texas, and in the second, pitched the Longhorns to a national championship. While in Austin, he fashioned a streak of 35 scoreless innings, an NCAA record that would stand for almost two decades.

At the time of his major league debut, knowledge of baseball prospects was reserved for scouts and others in the game. This was, of course, pre-internet, so there were no widely available videos online over which fans could drool. Even *Baseball America,* which would become the bible for amateur and minor league coverage of the game, was in its infancy and had limited reach and circulation.

But Clemens was known to even the casual Red Sox fans because he represented hope at a time when the major league club was thoroughly uninteresting. After their doomed 1978 playoff date with the Yankees, the Red Sox followed with a 91-win season in 1979 before entering a headlong slide into mediocrity.

The Sox were good enough to be over .500 most years, but in 1983, the year before Clemens' arrival, they suffered their first losing season since 1966. The 1983 season was also the final year in Yastrzemski's career, and his retirement left the franchise without much star power.

Into the vacuum strode Clemens, who made his debut on a raw night in Cleveland, before a sparse crowd. The results that night—5.2 innings, 11 hits allowed, four earned runs scored—were underwhelming. But there was something about his presence on the mound that promised more.

Clemens was built like a prototypical power pitcher. He stood 6'4" and weighed about 210 pounds. He owned a thick trunk, muscular legs, and a thunderbolt for a right arm.

He had something else, too, that couldn't be measured: a fiery disposition and a complete lack of fear. Like his hero Nolan Ryan, Clemens was unafraid to intimidate. He owned an explosive fastball that he could throw in the mid-90s and a devastating slider. (Clemens would later add a split-finger fastball to his arsenal, but at the start of his career was good enough to rely on mostly two pitches.)

As often happens with even the best prospects, his path to stardom was far from linear. In 1985, his second major league season, Clemens was discovered to have a torn labrum in his shoulder, requiring surgery.

Nervous Red Sox fans thought of other pitchers in franchise history whose careers were short-circuited by injuries and naturally feared the worst. But when a healthy Clemens returned in 1986, he quickly showed how unfounded their concerns were.

At the end of April, on a cold, unremarkable night at Fenway, Clemens put himself in the record books by striking out 20 Seattle Mariners, setting a Major League Baseball mark.

From the beginning, it was clear that Clemens was operating on a different plane that night. He fanned the side in the first, punched out two more in the second, added another in the third, and recorded the first two outs in the fourth. Seattle outfielder Gorman Thomas then hit a pop-up into foul territory.

The play was the definition of routine, but first baseman Don Baylor dropped the ball for an error, extending the at-bat for Thomas. But the misplay also gave Clemens a chance to record another strikeout, which he did. Baylor later denied that he intentionally misplayed the ball, but the circumstances made it appear highly suspicious.

Heading for the ninth, Clemens had 18 strikeouts and when he got former University of Texas teammate—and soon to be Red Sox teammate—Spike Owen swinging to start the inning, he tied a record held by four others, including Ryan, his idol.

One batter later, Clemens quickly separated himself from the group by getting Phil Bradley looking at a called third strike. With the crowd roaring for him to finish with one more, he got Ken Phelps on a groundout.

"The ninth inning," Clemens would say after the game, "was all adrenaline. I was just out there throwing."

The Mariners, meanwhile, were just out there swinging... and missing, again and again.

The dominance Clemens displayed that night—20 strikeouts, one run allowed on three hits, and remarkably, no walks—managed to whet everyone's appetite. Of his 20 whiffs, 12 were swinging and eight were called. He struck out everyone in the Mariners' lineup at least once, two batters twice, three others three times, and Bradley on four occasions.

"I've seen perfect games by Catfish Hunter and Mike Witt," said Sox manager John McNamara afterward, "and I've seen some great games pitched by [Tom] Seaver. But I've never seen a pitching performance as awesome as that and I don't think you will again in the history of baseball."

Added catcher Rich Gedman: "The thing that amazed me the most was that they had so many swings and weren't even able to foul the ball.... He was challenging them, and they weren't able to get a bat on the ball."

If Clemens could do this, in just his 40th major league start, in an otherwise nondescript setting, what else was he capable of?

The possibilities seemed limitless.

Clemens won his first 14 decisions in 1986, making for the best start to a season by a Red Sox starter in franchise history. It wasn't until July 2 that he was saddled with a loss. He was both dominant and incredibly durable—in his 15-game unbeaten streak to start the season, he failed to get into the eighth inning just twice.

He was the obvious choice to start the All-Star Game for the American League. Clemens tossed three shutout innings in an AL win and was chosen as the game's MVP.

At the age of 24, Clemens had announced his arrival on the scene.

He finished his first full season 24–4 with a 2.48 ERA and 238 strikeouts in 254 innings. He was, predictably, the unanimous choice for the AL Cy Young Award—the first for the franchise since Lonborg in 1967—and was named American League MVP, the first such honor for an AL starting pitcher since Vida Blue in 1971.

That postseason, the Red Sox's first in 11 years, Clemens proved himself to be human. In five starts—three in the thrilling ALCS triumph over the California Angels and two more in the World Series against the Mets—Clemens was rather ordinary, with a 3.97 ERA, winning just one of his five starts. (The team was 2–3 in his outings.)

Included in that workload was the controversial Game 6 start in the World Series. With the Sox ahead in the eighth inning and Clemens at a manageable 72 pitches, McNamara stunned everyone by pinch-hitting for Clemens in the top of the eighth.

When the Sox went on to lose in 10 innings, McNamara revealed that Clemens has asked out of the game after seven innings, citing a blister on his pitching hand. Clemens would forever dispute this account and insisted that he never requested to come out of the game.

Whatever the truth, a narrative emerged that October: that Clemens wasn't capable of winning when it counted most. It was an allegation that, fairly or not, would dog him for the rest of his time in a Red Sox uniform.

There was more ominous news next spring. Clemens walked out of spring training for three weeks in a contract dispute, unhappy with what he deemed a lowball offer. Eventually, the impasse was settled with a new two-year deal, but not before Red Sox GM Lou Gorman, asked his plans during his star pitcher's absence, famously responded: "The sun will come up, the sun will set, and I will have lunch."

The holdout resolved, Clemens had nonetheless alienated some fans with his actions. A fine 1987 season followed—another 20-win campaign and another Cy Young Award—but in 1988, his third full season, Clemens invited more displeasure from the fan base with his comments about the team failing to provide a secure seating area for family members, while complaining that the team made Sox players "carry [our] own bags" on road trips.

Clemens was attempting to use his status as the team's star player to improve conditions for teammates, but that wasn't how the remarks were taken by the public, who saw them as more evidence of how spoiled modern ballplayers were and, by extension, how entitled they had become.

From 1988 through 1992, Clemens won 92 more games—an average of 18 per year—and posted a 2.62 ERA, but twice more, the team stalled out in the postseason. In 1988 and again in 1990, the Sox fell to the Oakland A's in the ALCS.

In 1988, Clemens didn't pitch poorly—giving up three runs in seven innings—but then again, he didn't pitch his team to victory when it mattered most. In 1990, it got much worse. After losing a tough pitcher's duel to Dave Stewart—Clemens tossed six shutout innings, but Stewart outlasted him, allowing a run over eighth innings—Clemens got the ball again in Game 4 in Oakland, with the Sox facing elimination and a second humiliating sweep at the hands of the A's in the span of three seasons.

An amped-up Clemens—his face bearing so much eye black he looked to be auditioning for a role in *Braveheart,* and his cleats curiously tied by Teenage Mutant Ninja Turtles shoelaces—took exception to home plate Terry Cooney's strike zone early in the game. Jawing with Cooney, who ordered him to cease with the complaints about balls and strikes, Clemens became enraged, yelling at Cooney to "take off your fucking mask."

This earned him an ejection, which further sent Clemens over the edge. He had to be restrained from going after Cooney, while warning the umpire: "I know where you live!" A suspension by Major League Baseball predictably followed.

It was an unseemly display and further called into question Clemens' ability to handle the pressure of the postseason. What kind of All-Star got himself thrown out of a potential elimination game...*in the second inning?*

Clemens could be his own worst enemy when it came to public comments. In addition to his ill-advised remarks about the "inconveniences" experienced by highly paid pro athletes, he was often the master of malapropisms.

He once confessed to feeling "a little erotic [sic]" after having had extra rest between starts, and, on the occasion of Carl Yastrzemski's induction into Cooperstown, noted that the honor was "another nail in his coffin." (Presumably, he had meant to say "feather in his cap.")

For the next few seasons, Clemens continued to pitch like a top-of-the-rotation starter, winning a third Cy in 1991, but beginning in 1992, the team slid into a stretch of second-rate finishes under manager Butch Hobson.

For a time, Clemens maintained his All-Star-caliber pitching, cheated out of additional wins in 1992 due to either a lack of offensive support or a faulty bullpen.

In 1993, however, his performance began an unmistakable decline, resulting in a career-high 4.46 ERA. He rebounded in 1994, but in 1995, with the start of the season delayed by a labor dispute, he reported to camp out of shape and his pitching reflected that: he posted another bloated ERA (4.18).

In what turned out to be his final season with the Red Sox, Clemens, remarkably, notched another 20-strikeout game, this time against the Detroit Tigers.

As was the case the first time, Clemens didn't issue a single walk along the way. If anything, this outing may have been more impressive than the first. For one thing, Clemens didn't allow a run, earning his 38th career shutout. And the Tigers failed to get the ball out of the infield for the first five innings. And there was this: Clemens was 34 at the time.

When Clemens hit free agency after 1996—following something of a rebound season that saw him lead the league in strikeouts and finish with the seventh-best ERA and WHIP—general manager Dan Duquette made only a modest attempt to retain him, and when the pitcher signed with the Toronto Blue Jays, Duquette, in a public bit of passive-aggressiveness, observed that Clemens was "in the twilight of his career."

That fueled Clemens to no end. He returned to Fenway in a Toronto uniform the following summer and struck out 16 Red Sox, all the while staring down Duquette and managing general partner John Harrington in their suites as he walked off the mound.

Clemens would go to pitch through the 2007 season. No one could have imagined that he would have pitched nearly as many seasons elsewhere (11) as he had in Boston (13). And surely no one—Dan Duquette included—could have foreseen that he would win more Cy Young Awards (four) than he had while with the Red Sox (three).

Clemens would also go a long way toward changing the narrative of postseason failure. After earning one playoff or World Series win in nine starts for the Sox, Clemens was 7–4 in 17 postseason starts for the Yankees with a 3.24 ERA. Included in those: the Game 4 World Series clincher in 1999 against the Atlanta Braves, in which he allowed a single run over 7.2 innings.

Where, Red Sox fans had to be asking themselves, was *that* when he pitched for us?

His legacy remains a complicated one, both in Boston and elsewhere. Of pitchers born after 1900, only Warren Spahn and Greg Maddux have more wins. His seven Cy Young Awards have yet to be matched and may never be.

And, of course, there are the PED allegations. Though Clemens never tested positive for PEDs in his career and has steadfastly maintained his innocence, his name appeared prominently in the Mitchell Report and widespread suspicions have kept him out of the Hall of Fame.

Still, there can be little debate about his place in Red Sox history. He's tied—ironically, with Cy Young himself—for most wins and most shutouts by a pitcher in franchise history. Clemens alone owns the club record for most strikeouts and is first in WAR among pitchers.

Not all his impact can be measured via statistics. His presence gave the Red Sox a certain swagger that they had never experienced. Before Clemens, with few exceptions, it was usually the opposing team featuring the pitcher who instilled a mix of fear and awe. Clemens, for 13 seasons, changed that perception.

That the Sox never won it all during his stay cannot be held against him, any more than it can be held against Ted Williams or Yastrzemski or other legends who came before him. And there can be no doubting his competitiveness or will to win.

The Sox had waited for decades for a pitcher like Roger Clemens. When he left, there were recriminations and regrets, but little doubt about the contributions he had made. Finally, the Red Sox had known what it was like to have an honest-to-goodness, once-in-a-generation ace.

And perhaps here was the strangest thing: it would only take two more seasons for the next one to arrive.

14
Pedro Martinez

FOLLOWING (ALMOST) IMMEDIATELY IN THE FOOTSTEPS OF Roger Clemens, Pedro Martinez could not have been more different than his pitching predecessor.

Clemens was a big, strong Texan. Martinez was a slight, lean Dominican.

Clemens had the classic power pitcher build, an imposing physical presence supported by two tree trunks for legs.

Martinez gave the appearance that a stiff wind might blow him over. His original organization feared that he couldn't physically withstand the demands of being a starting pitcher in the big leagues.

Clemens was prone to long, rambling answers, full of nonsequiturs and malapropisms. Martinez, raised to speak Spanish, worked to command the English language as precisely as his pitches and showed remarkable fluency with his second language.

But they were not without some similarities.

Each was fiercely proud and relentlessly competitive. Each could be stubborn and occasionally capable of a mean streak on the mound. Neither thought twice about sending pointed messages via his lethal fastballs.

And there was this: each could make a compelling case that he was the best starting pitcher in modern Red Sox history. That one followed the other by just one season makes for a fascinating "what if" scenario: imagine the two had been teammates in Boston. How might that have changed the course of franchise history?

As it is, we're left with this: from 1984 through 2004, a period of better than 20 years, the Red Sox had, in all but one season (1997), one of the two best pitchers the game has ever known.

Martinez, unlike Clemens, did not begin his career with the Red Sox. He was acquired in one of the more lopsided trades in baseball history in November 1997, arriving via Canada, 11 months after Clemens had taken the reverse journey, spurning Boston for the Great White North, two pitching legends (nearly) passing in the night.

The loss of Clemens—and his subsequent brilliant first season in Toronto—may have led Red Sox GM Dan Duquette to pursue Martinez. Duquette had famously derided Clemens as being "in the twilight" of his career, only to have Clemens post one of his best seasons ever: 21–7, 2.05, a career-high 292 strikeouts, and the first of two consecutive pitching Triple Crowns.

Whatever the motivation, it was a brilliant trade. The Red Sox surrendered young pitchers Carl Pavano and Tony Armas for Martinez, fresh off winning the National League Cy Young Award. It marked the second time in his career that Duquette had traded for Martinez—five years earlier, he had stolen him for the Expos, from the Dodgers.

Duquette had seen how much the Red Sox missed having a legitimate No. 1 starter in 1997. The only Sox starter to make 30 or more starts that season was Aaron Sele, who compiled a 5.38 ERA as the Sox finished fourth in the five-team AL East, 20 games out of first place.

As a member of the Red Sox, Martinez was brilliant from the start. In 1998, he won 19 games and had a 2.89 ERA, good enough to finish second—irony alert—to Clemens in the Cy Young Award balloting. With the rotation bolstered by Martinez's presence, the Red Sox won 92 games and reached the postseason for the first time since 1995 before being ousted by Cleveland in the division series.

In 1999, Martinez was even better, winning 20 games for the first time (a career-best 23) and posting a 2.07 ERA. The Cy Young Award was a given, but Martinez probably deserved the AL MVP award, too. He lost out when a voter from New York inexplicably left him off his ballot altogether.

That season featured two starts that, separately, captured Martinez's obstinance and his brilliance.

In August, Martinez reported late to Fenway on a day in which he was supposed to start. Manager Jimy Williams, more than a little set in his ways himself, deemed this a violation of team rules and pulled Martinez from his scheduled start, replacing him with journeyman Bryce Florie.

Williams later inserted Martinez into the game and the tardy ace was the winning pitcher in relief.

Afterward, Martinez expressed regret for not notifying the team that he would be arriving later than usual but was incensed that Williams had publicly embarrassed him.

"Jimy had to prove he was the boss," said a seething Martinez, who had angrily confronted Williams in the dugout over the perceived slight.

A month later, it was the New York Yankees lineup that was late.

In one of the more masterful pitching performances anyone could recount, Martinez throttled a mighty Yankees lineup that was headed for a second straight championship the next month. He allowed a solo homer to Chili Davis with two out in the second inning and then didn't allow another baserunner the rest of the way, retiring the final 22 hitters he faced in succession. He finished the night with 17 strikeouts, no walks, and one hit allowed.

It was, on paper, every bit as impressive as either of the 20-strikeout performances by Clemens, and given the quality of the opposition, perhaps better. Neither the 1986 Seattle Mariners nor the 1996 Detroit Tigers were a match for the dynastic Yankee teams of the late 1990s.

October saw Martinez come out of Game 1 of the ALDS after four shutout innings with an upper back/shoulder strain as the Red Sox fell behind two games to none in the series. Gamely, the Sox battled back to take Games 3 and 4, and in the climactic Game 5, both teams came out swinging furiously.

Boston and Cleveland combined for 15 runs in the first three innings, like two heavyweights intent on landing an early knockout punch. When the Sox tied things in the top of the fourth, having already gone through two pitchers, they summoned Martinez in relief.

The moment the bullpen door swung open in right field at (then) Jacobs Field, a hush fell over the ballpark. In a matter of seconds, the crowd shifted from giddy to apprehensive. Until then, long-suffering Cleveland fans had felt good about their team's chances. But even a depleted Martinez had the potential to derail the Tribe.

No one—likely not even Martinez himself—knew what to expect from the pitcher and for how long. He hadn't appeared since Game 1 and was presumed out for the series, so the mere fact that he had been cleared to pitch at all caught most everyone off-guard.

If Martinez was harboring any self-doubt, he kept it hidden. With every eye trained on him throughout the ballpark, he jogged in breezily from right field, not an evident care in the world. This was baseball's biggest stage, the postseason in October, with his team embroiled in a winner-take-all elimination game. But to watch Martinez head for the mound, you could have easily mistaken it for a spring training game in March.

Then, just as Martinez approached the infield dirt, he stopped at the edge of the outfield cross and met with first base umpire Durwood Merrill. A veteran of better than 20 years, Merrill was 61 and sported a considerable paunch. Minutes before he was to take his team's fate in his hands on the mound, Martinez used those same hands to playfully rub Merrill's belly, like someone rubbing a statue of Buddha for good luck.

If Cleveland didn't already know it was in trouble, that should have convinced it otherwise. Limited by injury or not, Martinez was making sure everyone knew that he was not doubting himself.

What followed was a brilliant display of pitching. This wasn't vintage Pedro by any stretch—his fastball barely reached the high 80s—but Martinez was an artist that night, masterfully keeping the ball out of the middle of the plate and confounding a mighty Cleveland lineup that had scored a staggering 1,009 runs—the most by any team since in almost half a century—during the regular season.

Martinez relied heavily on breaking pitches and his changeup and spun six shutout, hitless innings.

"When you're in that situation," Martinez would tell MLB.com years later, "do or die, whatever resources you have, you have to use. And that's how I felt. I felt like I had to use every resource that I had. What was amazing was that the Indians never realized that I was hurt. They thought I was going to be the 98-mph guy that they were used to seeing and I never changed my approach and neither did they.

"It was changeups, breaking balls, little cutters, changeups, and my velocity was never there."

His heart and head were, however. That, combined with an altered delivery—Martinez lowered his arm angle to reduce the pressure on his ailing lat—was more than good enough.

Meanwhile, a three-run homer from Troy O'Leary in the seventh snapped an 8–8 tie and sent the Sox on to a 12–8 series-clinching victory and an ALCS date with the Yankees.

Technically, this would be the first time the Red Sox and Yankees had ever met in the postseason—the fabled 1978 game was actually an extension of the regular season—but the Sox weren't in the same class as their rivals, falling in five games.

Still, the one game the Sox won was, naturally, started by Martinez, who managed to easily outpitch—who else?—Clemens. By then, the discomfort Martinez felt in the back of his shoulder had greatly intensified to a stabbing ache.

Despite what he would later say was "the worst pain I've ever pitched in during a game," Martinez somehow managed to toss seven shutout innings, allowing two hits while striking out 12.

It would be the only Boston win of a one-sided series. But it would stand as evidence—if anyone still needed it—of Martinez's fierce will to compete, his mental toughness, and his artistry as a pitcher.

After two straight trips to the postseason, the 2000 season saw the Red Sox as a franchise regress. They finished just four games over .500, and the year was seen as a major disappointment. Except, of course, for Pedro, who enjoyed a season for the ages.

At a time when offensive production was at record levels across the game—due, in part, to the rampant use of PEDs—Martinez put up numbers that looked like they could have come from the Dead Ball Era. In 29 starts, he was 18–6 with a 1.74 ERA and 284 strikeouts in 217 innings. His WHIP was a cartoonish 0.737, the lowest in baseball history.

No stat, however, captures Martinez's dominance that season better than ERA+, or adjusted ERA. Designed to consider more variables—such as ballparks and opponents—it seeks to put a pitcher's performance into the context of its era. That season, Martinez's ERA+ was 291, meaning he was 191 percent better than the MLB average that season.

Historically, that was the best ERA+ recorded for a pitcher since 1900.

In other words, to put it in terms that are less analytical and more easily understood, Martinez was otherworldly and completely without peer that season.

Using more conventional stats, consider that while Martinez won the ERA title at 1.74, the next runner-up in the American League (Clemens) was at 3.70, *nearly two full runs higher.*

Dominant as he was, the numbers only tell half the story of Martinez's time in Boston.

In a way not seen before or since, the ballpark was transformed on days or nights when he pitched. The atmosphere was electric in anticipation. The mere sight of Martinez slowly strolling to the bullpen for his pregame warm-up, or later, to the mound for the top of the first, was enough to generate goose bumps. Who knew what you were going to be treated to that night?

Martinez also had the effect of diversifying the Fenway crowd. While the team had featured Latin superstars in the past, including the charismatic Luis Tiant, no one had the impact that Martinez had. It wasn't unusual for the ballpark to feature natives of the Dominican Republic, proudly waving the flag of their homeland, both in celebration of Martinez and as a means of proudly associating themselves with their compatriot.

Fenway, where, for too long, the players were exclusively white and which had been sadly hostile to players of color—both visiting and those on the home team—was suddenly proudly multicultural, with the vibrant atmosphere of a winter ball game in San Juan or Santo Domingo.

Martinez could not conceal the pride he took in drawing fans from the Latino community, though he was quick to tell anyone who would listen, in a lilting accent that made him sound like he had emigrated from Transylvania and not the DR, "I'm a Boss-TON-ian!"

Injuries limited Martinez to just a half-season workload in 2001, before he bounced back in 2002 and 2003 and more closely resembled his exceptional self. He was cheated out of what should have been his fourth Cy Young Award in 2002 and his 2003 was nearly as spectacular. Over the two seasons combined, he won 81 percent of his decisions and struck out 10.4 hitters per nine innings while averaging 193 innings.

Along the way, however, some cracks were showing between the Sox and Martinez. His original contract extension, signed soon after he was acquired from Montreal, was for six years and

$75 million with a club option for 2004 worth $15 million, plus bonuses. Martinez had pushed for the option to be picked up prior to the start of the 2003 season.

But talks on a longer extension past 2004 sputtered and the Sox took a few months before exercising their original 2004 option. Ever mindful of his worth and his own contributions, Martinez wasn't happy that the Sox took their time before executing the option and threatened to leave via free agency if the team didn't elect to pick up the deal.

Ownership had some concerns that Martinez was diminished by the shoulder issues he had suffered earlier, and their fears proved prophetic. Pitching in his age-32 season in 2004, Martinez would see his ERA skyrocket to 3.90, the highest of his career to that point.

By reputation and aura, he may have remained the team's ace, but he was outperformed that year—during the season and again in October—by new teammate Curt Schilling.

The two had a somewhat uneasy relationship, though ultimately there existed a mutual—if wary—respect between the two aces. Like many others in the game, Martinez felt that Schilling could be overbearing and pompous while Schilling regarded Martinez as diva-like. Neither was far off in his assessment.

As was his occasional habit, Martinez seemed intent on testing new manager Terry Francona by leaving the ballpark before the game concluded after a poor outing on Opening Night. The move put Francona in a bad light, suggesting that he didn't control his own clubhouse and players, but—not for the last time—the manager kept his anger from public view, defending Martinez despite the insubordination by insisting it was part of a misunderstanding.

As the season wore on, Martinez fretted about his unresolved contract status while upper management and ownership weighed the risks of committing tens of millions to a wildly popular pitcher who was, nonetheless, clearly in decline.

It was the ultimate tightrope to walk for the new ownership group led by John Henry, now in its third year.

With the Red Sox and Yankees battling it out for the American League East, with the Sox having gone 25–5 over a stretch of 30 late-season games, the result of a roster-altering blockbuster trade at the July deadline, the Sox had pulled to within two and a half games in September before the Yanks beat Martinez twice in the span of a week.

Seemingly frustrated by his struggles against New York, Martinez stunned baseball with a postgame expression of resignation. "What can I say, [but] just tip my hat and call the Yankees my daddy."

It may have been an overly candid assessment, but it was also most certainly un-Pedro-like. He was not one to publicly air what little self-doubt he harbored. Coming, as it did, after Martinez had failed to protect a lead in Game 7 of the ALCS the previous October, it was all the ammunition Yankee fans would need in the years ahead.

In his final major league appearance, as a member of the Philadelphia Phillies in 2009, Martinez would hear the "Who's your daddy?" taunts at Yankee Stadium. He had asked for them, in a way, with his crisis of confidence years earlier.

But first, he would get the last laugh with the Red Sox in October of 2004.

Martinez didn't pitch particularly well in the 2004 postseason. He allowed three runs in six innings in a Game 2 ALCS loss at Yankee Stadium before surrendering four runs over six in a Game 5 win.

The pitching center of attention was, instead, Schilling, who pitched brilliantly in Game 6 following a novel ankle procedure, resulting in the infamous "bloody sock."

With the Sox comfortably ahead 8–1 in Game 7 and cruising to a series win, Martinez pitched in mop-up and was knocked around for two runs on three hits, briefly injecting some life into the Yankee Stadium crowd, who could be forgiven, considering the history of the rivalry, for thinking that Martinez's relief stint signaled the start of a late-game comeback.

It was not to be this time, but this inglorious relief appearance served as a discomfiting coda, the next-to-last appearance in Martinez's magnificent career in Boston.

He rallied to make a more fitting contribution in the World Series, shutting out the St. Louis Cardinals for seven innings in Game 3, then enjoyed the celebration on the field and in the clubhouse and the duck boat parade to the fullest.

It was Martinez's swan song. A new contract agreement could not be reached, and in the wake of their historic World Series win, the team and its most magnetic pitcher ever parted ways, none too amicably.

In retrospect, given Martinez's performance over his final five seasons elsewhere (four with the New York Mets and a half-season with the Phillies), it was the right call. But there was something undeniably sad that this storybook tale—of a pitcher who attained unimaginable heights and shone so brightly for his seven seasons—could not have had a happier ending.

For a time, Martinez's acrimonious departure harkened back to an earlier era, when every Red Sox star—from Carlton Fisk to Fred Lynn to Wade Boggs to Clemens—left in a fit of pique. But after his playing career, Martinez and the team mended things and he returned as a special assistant and semi-regular presence at Fenway.

Martinez's main role is to work with the organization's young pitching prospects, some of whom, especially the Latinos, regard him with a mixture of awe and wonderment. The hope is, however fanciful it may be, that some of the magic that he visited upon the franchise is transferrable and that someday, a bit of his genius might manifest itself in the arm of another.

Call it wishful thinking. As anyone who had the privilege to watch Martinez in a Red Sox uniform will confirm, there will never be another like him.

PART 6

JUST MISSED

15

1967

FOR MANY CURRENT-DAY RED SOX FANS, THE MODERN era begins in 2004, when 86 years of futility finally—and mercifully—came to an end.

That is a natural enough perspective. After 2004, long-suffering fans could hold their heads high and were no longer subjected to taunts of "1918," the last season that had ended with the Red Sox being crowned champions.

In actuality, for those with longer memories and fan pedigrees, the modern era begins in 1967. Unlike 2004—or the three subsequent championships that followed over the next 14 years—that year did conclude with a title. But for many, it is the year in which Red Sox history, like the dream sequence in *The Wizard of Oz,* transitions from black-and-white to color.

Indeed, some 55 years later, the 1967 season represents a kind of demarcation. No other season—not 1919, the first year without Babe Ruth; not 1939, the first season to feature Ted

Williams—more completely defines the "before-and-after" element in Red Sox history.

It's easy to now forget that, prior to 1967, the Red Sox had transitioned into perennial losers, known more for a few fabulous star players than any collective achievement. In the early 1960s, their inability to even sniff contention resulted in such a massive drop-off in attendance that Thomas A. Yawkey fretted about the franchise's viability.

For decades, Yawkey had been the embodiment of the mid-century sportsman/owner, indulging himself with high-salaried teams as if to satisfy his own whimsy. The Red Sox were an expensive hobby for Yawkey, and he treated his players as a benevolent boss would. He wasn't above sharing a cigar with a star player or taking part in the occasional round of pepper before a game.

If the Red Sox won, great. And if they didn't, well, it sure was nice to be the sole owner of a major league baseball team.

But after Williams retired in 1960, the franchise began an especially fallow period. The team was often run by managers for whom drinking was far more important than winning, and unsurprisingly, the win-loss record often reflected that.

Also unsurprising was the team's inability to attract fans.

Even as the Red Sox spent the entire 1950s without winning a pennant, the team routinely drew one million fans. But by the mid-1960s, nine straight losing seasons had completely tested the local fandom's patience—to say nothing of their disposable income. In 1965, the Sox drew just 652,201, their lowest total since World War II.

Yawkey worried that Fenway, already more than half a century old and very much showing its age, could not attract fans and privately investigated a move out of the city, where land was far cheaper and parking more plentiful—the better to capitalize on the era's migration to the suburbs.

Reflecting the tumult of the era, the Red Sox had cycled through eight managers in the previous nine seasons. For 1967, they summoned a 40-year-old minor league manager, Dick Williams, who had spent the previous few seasons overseeing the organization's best prospects.

In the mold of so many managers of the era—Walter Alston, Ralph Houk, Bill Rigney—Williams had had an unremarkable playing career in the majors, playing for five teams over the course of 13 seasons. But like the others, Williams had made good use of his time as a spare part—watching the game with a more critical eye, examining strategy, and absorbing the finer points of managing a roster.

When Williams arrived for spring training in Winter Haven, Florida, he got everyone's attention quickly.

First, he made what seemed like an outlandish vow: "I know one thing—we'll win more than we lose."

To those who were still paying attention, Williams might have been more believable had he announced his intention to fill his Opening Day starting lineup with nine little green men from outer space.

From where was this optimism flowing? Surely not from the team that, only the season prior, had finished ninth in a 10-team league, a full 26 games out of first.

But Williams, having managed the Triple A team in Toronto in 1965–66 and finishing first both times, had had a firsthand look at the future. He knew the talent that had been fermenting in the system and was now ready to contribute at the big-league level.

Perhaps more than anything, however, Williams had an abiding faith in himself. He seemed to know instinctually that he could get the most out of players—old and young alike—and figured his authoritarian manner could whip the roster into a more disciplined unit.

From the start of spring training, Williams demanded attention to detail. Gone was the country club atmosphere that had suffused the franchise with the stench of entitlement—a byproduct, one supposes, of the owner's benevolence. Before Williams, stars like Yastrzemski answered to no one; upon the arrival of the rookie manager, there was suddenly a culture of accountability.

Next, as if to exercise his authority, he stripped Yastrzemski of the captaincy, a not-so-subtle reminder that Williams—and only Williams—was in charge.

Spring training found the Red Sox uncharacteristically focused on fundamentals and conditioning. From now on, the Red Sox would pay attention to the details and execution—the little things that can, by themselves, turn an also-ran into a more respectable outfit.

Williams himself refused to settle or limit his expectations. He demanded more of his club than they had asked of themselves, in part because no one had pushed them before. By contrast, Williams pushed—hard at times. There were fines for failing to hustle, for missing a sign or missing a cutoff man. More than his own brashness—which itself was considerable—Williams brought to the job a quality that had for too long been absent: a demand for responsibility.

The results were obvious almost immediately. Although the Red Sox were just three games over .500 at the end of June, the very fact that they remained in contention halfway through the season was achievement enough—particularly for a team that had finished next-to-last the year before.

In July the team's growing confidence was further spurred by a 10-game winning streak that culminated with consecutive road series sweeps of Baltimore and Cleveland. When the team returned from that road swing, an adoring crowd of several thousand welcomed them back to Logan Airport.

A horrific beaning of Tony Conigliaro on August 11 cost the Red Sox their outfielder for the remainder of the season and nearly cost the Massachusetts native his career. Conigliaro was struck in the face by an errant pitch from California Angels pitcher Jack Hamilton and the sickening sound of the impact turned Fenway into hushed silence.

At the time, Conigliaro was second on the team to Yastrzemski in OPS and slugging percentage and third in homers.

Still, the Sox soldiered on, starting a seven-game winning streak on the night of the Conigliaro tragedy.

No retelling of the 1967 season is complete without special focus on Yastrzemski.

The '67 season was his seventh with the Red Sox, and while he won the American League batting title in 1963 with a .321 average and was a three-time All-Star selection, there was nothing—nothing—to suggest he was capable of what he accomplished in 1967.

The foundation was laid the previous winter, when Yastrzemski dedicated himself to an intense training regimen that included weightlifting. Today, such a workout program would be considered routine, but at the time, it was virtually unheard of.

Whatever Yastrzemski did to his body in the offseason, it resulted in a remarkable transformation. Only once, in his first year, had Yastrzemski hit as many as 20 homers in a season, and in the early going, his power hadn't spiked, with just two homers in the first 25 games.

But the conditioning work was meant to prepare Yastrzemski for the demands of the long season, and as the season progressed, he maintained his strength. Hardly a powerhouse physically at 5'11" and 175 pounds, Yastrzemski seemingly got stronger over the course of the year.

He would need that, since, at times, the outfielder was figuratively carrying the team on his back. While some young stars—first baseman George Scott, shortstop Rico Petrocelli, and Conigliaro, until he was sidelined—made contributions, the Sox were, at bottom, heavily dependent on Yaz.

Beyond his gaudy numbers, which translated into winning the Triple Crown—a feat no American Leaguer would duplicate for the next 45 seasons—it wasn't always merely what Yastrzemski did, but when. If the Red Sox needed a big hit, he provided it. If they needed a game-saving catch (or throw), he made that, too.

In the first week of the season, Yastrzemski saved a no-hitter—for a time, anyway—in Yankee Stadium for rookie lefty Billy Rohr, who was making his major league debut. Leading off the ninth inning, New York outfielder Tom Tresh hit a rocket to left center. Yastrzemski bolted after it, hurtled himself airborne, and, as TV announcer Ken Coleman described in astonishment, "came down with that ball."

Decades later, Yastrzemski, never comfortable discussing his own feats, was asked if the catch was the best of his 23-year career.

"Considering the circumstances," the Hall of Famer said, "yes, it was."

It was also symbolic of what was to come. Throughout the season, Yastrzemski would materialize, seemingly out of nowhere, like Superman intervening at a time of crisis. Batting third, he anchored the lineup. Patrolling left, he would supply circus catches, playing Fenway's Green Monster with an expertise that bordered on the miraculous. Yastrzemski seemed to know each square foot of The Wall as one would know the contours of one's own hand.

Frequently, he would play caroms barehand, the better to position himself for a quick, accurate strike back to the infield, or, if necessary, to the plate. Sometimes, his quick reactions discouraged baserunners from advancing in the first place; at others, they foolishly tempted fate and were met with a harsh tag at second or home plate, another rally snuffed out before it could begin.

Yastrzemski, with the dramatic sense of a superhero, seemed to save his best for last. In September, as a handful teams jockeyed for position and attempted to elbow their way to first, Yastrzemski was otherworldly—in the final 27 games of the regular season, each one critical to the Red Sox, Yastrzemski compiled a slash line of .417/.504/.760 with nine homers and 26 RBI.

And within that month, Yastrzemski somehow found the wherewithal to elevate his game still further on the season's final weekend. In the last two games of the most intense pennant race imaginable, Yaz was 7-for-8 with six RBI.

If Yastrzemski was the team's—and the league's—MVP, then Jim Lonborg was their pitching savior.

A total of a dozen pitchers started games for the Red Sox that season, from journeyman Gary Bell to veteran holdover Dave Morehead to rookie Ken Brett. But none had anywhere near the impact Lonborg had.

Nothing in Lonborg's first two seasons in the majors (a combined 19–27, 4.17) suggested he had that kind of season in him. Lanky and handsome and a graduate of Stanford, Lonborg was soft-spoken and earned the nickname "Gentleman Jim," a sobriquet that was partly ironic given that Lonborg was hardly the picture of chivalry on the mound.

To the contrary, Lonborg was an intense competitor, unafraid to claim the inside of the plate for himself and more than willing to deliver pointed messages from 60 feet six inches. Earlier in the season, Lonborg watched as his third baseman, Joe Foy, was struck by a pitch in the helmet and calmly exacted his revenge by drilling Yankee starter Thad Tillotson in the back, igniting a bench-clearing brawl that lasted more than five minutes.

But Lonborg's role went well beyond handing down his own peculiar brand of frontier justice. When he wasn't having his teammates' backs, he was establishing himself as the staff's ace. He logged a staggering 273.1 innings and recorded 15 complete games.

And like Yastrzemski, Lonborg demonstrated the ability to rise to the occasion. The more important the outing, the better he was. In the final stretch, in his final 10 games of the regular season, Lonborg was 6–3 with a 2.31 ERA.

On the final day of the season, he tossed a complete game in which he allowed just one earned run and jumpstarted a sixth-inning rally by dropping down a near-perfect bunt.

* * *

September brought with it arguably the greatest conclusion to a pennant race in the post-expansion era. Just one and a half games separated four teams—the Red Sox, Minnesota Twins, Detroit Tigers, and Chicago White Sox—with just four days to go in the regular season. A two-game sweep of the Twins on the final weekend, coupled with a win by the California Angels over the Tigers, clinched the Red Sox's first pennant since 1946.

A date with the St. Louis Cardinals—ironically enough, also the franchise's opponent when it had last reached the World Series 21 years earlier—beckoned.

From the start, the Sox were poorly positioned from a pitching standpoint. Because the Sox had needed their ace, Lonborg, to pitch the final game of the regular season, he was unable to start Game 1 of the World Series and match up with the incomparable Bob Gibson.

The Cardinals won the opener, despite a strong start (and a home run) from Red Sox starter Jose Santiago.

Lonborg was brilliant in his first two starts. In Game 2, he allowed two baserunners—one on a single, another on a walk—in a complete-game shutout; in Game 5, he allowed a solo run on three hits and once more went the distance.

His first two starts, then: 18 innings, one earned run, four hits, and one walk allowed.

But the Sox eventually ran out of runway. When a winner-take-all Game 7 materialized, the Cards had Gibson on regular rest while the Red Sox were forced to start Lonborg with just two days' rest. Somewhat predictably, with Lonborg heroically operating on fumes, the Sox were no match for Gibson's brilliance, dropping Game 7 to the Cards—exactly as their predecessors had done in the 1946 Series.

The loss was hugely disappointing, of course, and left the team a win shy of achieving its ultimate goal. At the time, however, despite the incessant obsession with curses and decades without a championship to show, the setback wasn't seen as calamitous, or any kind of karmic manifestation. That would come later.

A half-century later, in fact, some prominent players expressed their acceptance of the team's second-best status.

"If I was a writer," mused Lonborg of falling just short, "I would have written that into the script."

16
1975

The gap between the next pennant-winning edition of the Red Sox and the last one—a mere eight seasons—was nowhere near as long as the one between the two previous.

Still, a lot had happened to the franchise—and the city—since the Impossible Dream season. Following the firing of Dick Williams in the final week of the 1969 season, Eddie Kasko had been named manager, and while he guided the club to three straight winning seasons, he, too, was dismissed after 1973 and replaced by Darrell Johnson.

Like Williams and Kasko, his immediate (full-time) predecessors, Johnson had spent time in the Red Sox minor league system, having managed the team's Triple A affiliate. The hope was that Johnson's familiarity with the organization's younger players would result in a smooth transition for all.

But the 1975 season was a time of transition for both the Red Sox and the industry.

For decades, baseball had dominated the American sports landscape. Its star players were also the country's most recognizable athletes. The World Series was annually the biggest sporting event on the calendar.

But domination of the American sports scene was a cyclical business and, already, some previously popular industries were beginning to fade.

Horse racing was the most obvious example. Once in the upper echelon of attractions, racing had begun to fade, failing to attract younger fans as its older ones died off. The 1970s would feature three Triple Crown winners—Affirmed, Seattle Slew, and the unparalleled Secretariat—but the number of tracks closing down during the decade began to escalate while attendance at the remaining tracks slipped.

The same could be said for boxing. Muhammad Ali's return to the ring following a three-year exile while he fought induction into the Army injected the sport with arguably its most compelling figure, and Ali's three fights with rival Joe Frazier and his memorable "Rumble in the Jungle" championship bout with George Foreman represented record paydays and heightened fan interest.

But across the sport, boxing was fading. While Ali sucked up all the oxygen, the other weight classes receded into the background. The sport became less mainstream, and the arrival of pay-per-view as a business model removed fights from traditional broadcast television—at least in terms of live telecasts. TV still brought the biggest fights into the American living rooms, but now, it did so a week or so after the fight took place, usually as part of ABC's *Wide World of Sports.*

The diminution of horse racing and boxing—though they were still profitable and appealing—was a reminder that America's love affair with certain sports was fickle. Fans—and their disposable income and TV viewing time—could move on and find new interests. Popularity in the 1950s and 1960s didn't necessarily translate to a lifetime of devotion.

Fans were free to change their habits, casting aside one sport for another. And whether baseball realized it or not, it, too, was vulnerable to the whims of the American sports consumer.

To be sure, baseball was still wildly popular. The All-Star Game was the crown jewel of the summer sports calendar, offering fans a then-rare glimpse of stars from the "other" league. At the time, the National League and American League held actual separate identities. The National League was viewed as the more athletic of the two, with an emphasis on base stealing and speed, while the American League was more traditional and more reliant on power.

The National League was more fastball-heavy, while pitchers in the American League were more likely to rely on breaking pitches. And there was a distinct difference in ballparks—while the American League featured historic playgrounds like Fenway Park, Yankee Stadium, and Tiger Stadium, the National League was busy transitioning into newer, all-purpose stadia, often with symmetrical dimensions and artificial turf.

There were separate league offices, separate umpiring crews, and separate identities. You were either a fan of one or the other—not both. And those cleavages only resulted in heightened interest on the two annual occasions when the leagues met on the field—at the midsummer All-Star Game and again in the fall for the World Series.

But even baseball's hold on the sports fan was beginning to slip. Two labor disputes had impacted the 1972 and 1973 seasons—the first because of the strike and the second, while resulting in no lost games, because of a lockout.

The idea of pro athletes being represented by unions struck many as wrong-headed, and the cancellation of 86 games in 1972 left some alienated. Wasn't sport supposed to offer an escape from the drudgery of everyday life? Weren't the games supposed to serve as a distraction from the real world?

And yet, here were games being wiped out by the same forces that resulted in garbage strikes or walkouts by auto workers. For some, it was too much.

At the same time, football began an encroachment into baseball's dominance. It began, as was so often the case with any changes to the culture, with TV.

Baseball had grown as a radio sport. It existed in the background if need be—faintly from the other room, quietly from underneath a child's pillow past bedtime, or as a companion in the car, at the beach, or at a backyard barbeque.

Its schedule required a daily investment of time and a six-month commitment. Baseball, for all its inherent charm, could be demanding.

Football, by contrast, was different. With games played weekly instead of daily, it was more casual in its need for attention. A three-hour window—on the weekend, no less—wasn't much to ask of its fans.

And when football took the dramatic step of staging Monday night games in 1970, it changed American viewing habits forever. Suddenly, there was a bonus game to attract viewers who weren't quite sated with their football fix from the weekend, who needed one more serving before the next weekend.

It didn't matter that it likely wasn't your team being featured. Football's innate appeal to gamblers was undeniable, attracting those who didn't have a rooting interest and providing, instead, a financial one. And for those who had taken a beating with their bets on the previous day, *Monday Night Football* offered one last chance to get even for the week.

The concept of *Monday Night Football* took some time to succeed. But eventually, it became habit-forming for fans—perfectly positioned on a night in which little else was available—and soon became a dominant ratings winner for ABC.

MNF became appointment viewing and opened the door for the NFL to realize its ascension.

Baseball, king of the sports landscape for decades, unchallenged as America's Pastime, was slowly but inexorably losing its stranglehold as the country's No. 1 game.

But before the transfer was complete, before football so obviously eclipsed it as the country's top sport, baseball had one last statement to make: the 1975 World Series.

The 1975 season was a year of transition for the Red Sox.

While the 1975 roster featured a couple of stubborn holdouts from the 1967 Impossible Dream Team—Carl Yastrzemski and Rico Petrocelli—and a Cuban expat amid an improbable late-career renaissance (Luis Tiant), the 1975 season was driven by the arrival of a handful of young homegrown stars who would form the nucleus of the Sox for a handful of seasons to come.

Two outfielders, as different as could be, led the way.

Jim Rice and Fred Lynn could not be more different. Rice was Black, and Lynn was white. Rice hit righthanded, while Lynn hit from the left side. Rice was drafted out of high school from the South, while Lynn was a college star from the University of Southern California.

One was imbued with raw strength and power, muscling balls over Fenway's inviting left field wall. The other was smoother, peppering the same wall with a sweet stroke while making acrobatic catches across Fenway's expansive center field.

Together, they enjoyed spectacular rookie seasons. Rice hit .309 with 22 homers and 102 RBI, while Lynn bettered those spectacular numbers, batting .331 with 21 homers and 105 RBI, to go with 47 doubles and 103 runs scored—both tops in the league.

Lynn became the first player to be voted Rookie of the Year and Most Valuable Player, but together, their contributions—and at such young ages—marked them as foundational pieces for the franchise.

They were nicknamed the Gold Dust Twins, and it appeared as though, together, they would be the contrasting faces of the franchise.

They were not alone in their youth and talent. The Red Sox farm system, long one of the game's most fruitful development systems, was churning out young players like some sort of baseball assembly line.

Catcher Carlton Fisk, a New Englander by birth, had been named AL Rookie of the Year and had evolved into a perennial All-Star at 27. Dwight Evans, who would be the rare example of a player who was better in his thirties than his twenties, was another homegrown everyday position player, rounding out the outfield with Lynn and Rice.

And at shortstop, the Sox featured an ornery and intense 24-year-old who, though a native of the Golden State, was the very antithesis of California cool. Rick Burleson was so uber-competitive that teammate Bill Lee famously said of him, "Some guys don't like to lose, but Rick got angry if the score was even tied."

On most nights, the 1975 Red Sox could field homegrown players in all but one of the nine spots in the lineup—only journeyman second baseman Denny Doyle, who shared time at the position with Doug Griffin, was not drafted and developed by the Red Sox.

In the years to come, hodgepodge rosters assembled from other teams would become commonplace. But even in the pre-free agent era, such homogeneity was rare and a shining testament to the Red Sox's scouting and development success.

The 1974 Red Sox had folded badly down the stretch. Emerging from a slow start in late May, the Red Sox sat in either first or second place for much of the late spring and into the summer, never more than a game or so off the pace.

In late August, the Sox led the division by as many as seven games. But in what would be a bit of foreshadowing of the 1978 season, September saw the club nosedive, unable to reverse its free fall. On the first of September, the Red Sox had first place to themselves, albeit with a modest two-game lead.

A little over four weeks later, they had tumbled out of first, overtaken by not one but two teams, and settled for a third-place finish, with a 12–18 record in the final month.

The 1975 season began with optimism. Rice and Lynn had gotten their feet wet as September call-ups, though, of course, no one could have foreseen the degree to which they would dominate the American League in their first full seasons.

The Sox moved into first place in late June and, like some house guest overstaying their welcome, wouldn't be dislodged. The team didn't spend a single day out of first the rest of the way and won the division handily.

An American League Championship Series date with the dynastic Oakland A's looked to be an imposing matchup. The A's, full of stars and owned (and dominated) by eccentric owner Charlie Finley, had won three straight World Series and a fourth seemed eminently reachable.

But the Red Sox got little resistance from the A's. In the opener of the best-of-five series, the ageless Tiant tossed a complete-game three-hitter. In the second game, the Sox broke open a 3–3 game with single runs in the sixth, seventh, and eighth—all of them off Hall of Fame reliever Rollie Fingers, who, incredibly, pitched the final four innings.

The A's, pushed to the brink, returned home but not even the comforts of the dank Oakland–Alameda County Coliseum could save them from elimination—worse, by a sweep, ending their title run in most ignominious fashion.

That led to a showdown with the National League champion Cincinnati Reds, known ominously as the Big Red Machine.

Across seven games and 12 days—thanks to October rain showers that postponed one game for three straight days—the Red Sox and Reds conducted a Series for the ages.

The Series featured a little bit of everything, not the least of which was star power. Together, the two teams would produce six Hall of Famers—Yastrzemski, Rice, and Fisk from the Boston side, with Johnny Bench, Tony Perez, and Joe Morgan from Cincinnati.

The ageless Tiant spun a complete-game five-hit shutout in the opener before the Reds got even in Game 2.

It also had controversy, never a bad thing when it came to generating viewer interest. In Game 3, the Reds' Ed Armbrister appeared to have interfered with Fisk on a sacrifice bunt try, but home plate umpire Larry Barnett refused to call the infraction, earning himself an ignominious place in New England sports lore, right alongside NFL referee Ben Dreith, who, a year later, would kill the Patriots' Super Bowl chances with a phantom roughing the passer penalty against Ray Hamilton.

Back and forth these teams battled, exchanging taut wins and figurative blows. Of the seven games, five were decided by a single run, including two that went to extra innings. In four of the seven, the winning run was scored in the final at-bat by the victorious team.

Just to add to the tension, rain wiped out the scheduled Game 6 for three consecutive days, drenching the Fenway lawn while whetting everyone's appetite for more.

When Game 6 was finally played, it did not disappoint.

In fact, a strong case could be made that Game 6, won by the Red Sox in 12 innings when Carlton Fisk clanged a home run off the left field foul pole, is the greatest World Series game of all time. It featured a number of lead changes, 12 different pitchers, and all seven of the Red Sox runs scoring via homers, including two of the most famous in World Series history.

Bernie Carbo contributed a thrilling pinch-hit three-run homer in the bottom of the eighth to forge a 3–3 tie before both teams saw their powerful lineups go into hibernation for the next three innings.

The tension was palpable. At one point, Pete Rose dug into the batter's box before turning to Fisk, squatting in anticipation, and noting, "This is some kind of game, isn't it?"

It was rare, for the era, for the players to "break character" and acknowledge the competition with opponents. And that would be particularly true for Rose, the ultimate on-field warrior and well-known hard-ass who once barreled over an opposing catcher in an All-Star contest. For Rose, winning was life-and-death. But even he was moved to remark on the drama in which the players found themselves.

A few innings later, Fisk would end it with a majestic swing of the bat, swatting at a 1-0 offering from reliever Pat Darcy and driving it into the night. The only question was whether the ball would stay fair.

As he moved out of the batter's box following his swing, Fisk attempted to will the ball fair, "pushing" the ball with both arms as if swatting away a giant bug. The iconic footage was captured by NBC cameras, stationed inside Fenway's famed Green Monster. The TV coverage of the game was nearly as memorable as the game itself.

"There it goes.... There's a long drive...if it stays fair.... Home run!" said play-by-play voice Dick Stockton, in a call that managed to be, at once, sparse and descriptive.

Could Game 7 match that? Not quite. Still, it had its moments. Heading into the sixth, the Red Sox led 3–0, and there was hope— however foreign that concept was at the time to Red Sox fans—that the long drought would soon be over.

Just three more innings.

Of course, it didn't work out that way. Bill Lee threw an Eephus pitch—repurposed as a "Leephus" pitch—a lazy, looping breaking ball that looked like something you might see in a slow-pitch softball tournament—that Perez nearly hit into Kenmore Square.

An inning later, an RBI single from Rose knotted things at 3–3, which is how it stayed until the ninth. Johnson made the curious decision to go with rookie Jim Burton in the ninth, a move that soon backfired. A soft line single to center by Morgan scored Ken Griffey with the go-ahead run.

The Sox went down without much of a fight in the bottom of the inning, with Yastrzemski—as he would do three seasons later in the 1978 playoff game against the Yankees—making the final out.

At the time, the compelling nature of the games partly obscured the disappointment of defeat for the Red Sox. Some wishful Red Sox fans, with the benefit of hindsight, had suggested that Game 7 be stricken from the record books with the Series officially declared a tie.

While the proposal was hopelessly naïve, it had a degree of merit. In a World Series so compelling, so hard-fought, and so artfully played, neither team deserved to lose.

The Series also served to rejuvenate the sport for a time and serve as a reminder of how great the game could be—absent the labor woes and the impending shakeup that would be caused by the arrival of free agency.

Football's inexorable march toward sports supremacy couldn't be stopped altogether, but the majesty of the 1975 World Series served to slow it down some.

But neither baseball nor life works that way. Red Sox fans had to be content with the memories of Tiant twirling on the mound and Fisk pirouetting down the first-base line—a dream frozen in Game 6 time, before the harsh realities of Game 7 interceded.

It would be 11 long years before the Sox returned to the Fall Classic. Red Sox fans couldn't have known that the ending to that one would be, somehow, uglier and more painful.

17

1986

By 1986, it wasn't funny anymore.

In each of the two previous decades, the Red Sox had had the misfortune of meeting the best National League team of that particular decade in the World Series, and, both times, losing in a seventh game.

The St. Louis Cardinals had the best record of any NL champion of the 1960s, and the combination of Bob Gibson and an athletic St. Louis lineup proved too much for the Impossible Dreamers.

Still, because that Red Sox season was such an unexpected delight, because it had come out of nowhere, it was hard to feel cheated by the World Series result.

There was lingering disappointment, to be sure. What if Jim Lonborg had gone into the Series fully rested, able to match up with Gibson on a more level playing field? What if the Sox had had Tony Conigliaro in their lineup, providing them with one more dangerous hitter in a batting order that had come to rely so heavily on Carl Yastrzemski?

But the questions mostly receded into the background. The 1967 Sox had energized New England, made the Red Sox relevant again. And surely there was no shame in losing out to Gibson, one of the sport's most ardent competitors with a reputation as an unmatched big game performer.

As for the disappointment of 1975, that, too, was mitigated.

The Sox, having dominated one dynasty to reach the Fall Classic, fell short against another. The Big Red Machine were in the middle of a decade in which they won four pennants and two World Series, and lost in the National League Championship Series two other times. Losing to them was no shame.

And for many Red Sox fans, the glow of the Game 6 victory nearly—*nearly*—made up for losing the Series.

The Series itself—with five of the games decided by one run, two of them in extra innings and four games determined in the winning team's final at-bat—was judged a classic, one of the handful of best ever, by historians.

The lasting images associated with the Series—highlighted by Carlton Fisk willing the ball fair in the 12th inning—were seared into the memories of baseball fans everywhere.

Again, the disappointment was palpable. Again, the Sox had fallen a win short. But Red Sox fans had reason to believe that, with a roster featuring homegrown stars still in their twenties, more deep runs into October would happen soon enough.

They did not, however. And when the team forfeited three of those star players—trading Rick Burleson and Fred Lynn and losing Fisk on a contractual technicality—the bitterness began to percolate.

Worse, for Red Sox fans, was the recognition that their team, one of the charter franchises of the American League, had gone decades without a title. When other historic franchises like the Dodgers and Cardinals—even the hated Yankees—won, it was a little easier to accept.

But the 1980s saw one-time expansion teams like the Kansas City Royals and San Diego Padres reaching the World Series, then Boston's championship drought began to feel like a burden.

Suddenly, the near-misses in 1967 and 1975 and 1978 were no longer enough. There may have been a romance to coming close, to watching what seemed like certain victory snatched away at the last minute, like Lucy once more pulling the football away from a hapless Charlie Brown.

But by the mid-1980s, all of that had lost its luster. Just when it appeared that the Red Sox could not find yet another way to cruelly taunt their long-suffering fan base, they would find a new one.

At least, some thought, the Chicago Cubs, the closest Red Sox approximation the National League had to offer, had the good sense to be plain bad and irrelevant. They didn't take their fans on a wild joy ride, only to crash the car just inches from the finish line. No, the Cubs stalled out long before things got interesting.

The Cubs didn't bother pretending. They didn't so much as win a pennant from 1945 for the rest of the 20th century. When it came to dashing the hopes of their fans, the Cubs had the good manners to quit while they were behind.

Not so the Red Sox. And in many ways, the 1986 campaign would be the cruelest taunt yet.

At the start of the 1986 season, expectations were modest. The Red Sox hadn't sniffed the postseason in more than a decade. The 1978 defeat at the hands of the Yankees seemed to suck the life out of the club for a few years.

Don Zimmer, ultimately if unfairly, paid for the '78 disappointment with his job in the final week of the 1980 season. Zimmer had averaged almost 96 wins in his first three years, but the cloud of '78 hung over him like the sword of Damocles. From the time the final out was made that October afternoon at Fenway, Zimmer's fate was cast.

Skewered by local talk shows, ridiculed for his resemblance to Popeye, and painted as the face of the game's most infamous second-half collapse, his termination was only a matter of time.

Four years of Ralph Houk followed, and if ever an era of modern Red Sox baseball could be labeled as nondescript, it was this one. Houk had managed the New York Yankees to two championships and a pennant in his three seasons on the job, but that proved illusory. Over the next 13 seasons as a major league manager—eight more with the Yankees after a two-year hiatus, followed by five more in Detroit—Houk never won anything again.

That ignominy followed Houk to Boston, where he played the role of placeholder. In his early sixties and three years removed from his last dugout gig, Houk sometimes appeared to be merely playing out the string, and his team reflected that.

To replace Houk after 1984, the Sox turned to John McNamara, who had earlier crossed paths with Haywood Sullivan, then the team's managing general partner. McNamara was 53 at the time of his appointment, though, with gray hair and bulbous nose, could have passed for at least a decade older.

His managerial career had already lasted nine full seasons and parts of two others and had been marked without much distinction. He had posted winning records just four times.

McNamara had been revered by his Black players while managing in the minors because he stood up on their behalf to segregationist efforts in the South in the 1960s. Beyond that, he offered little, and his hiring by a long-ago association only reinforced the notion that McNamara was the embodiment of the Old Boy Network.

One thing that McNamara had going for him, however, was a talented roster. In his first season, he oversaw a club that finished exactly at .500. Much of that team—including a productive if aging outfield trio of Jim Rice, Tony Armas, and Dwight Evans, as well as in-his-prime Wade Boggs at third—returned for 1986, but there were a few important additions.

Right before the season started, the Sox swapped veteran DHs with the Yankees, acquiring the righthanded Don Baylor for the lefty-swinging Mike Easler. Known for his leadership ability, Baylor brought a voice of accountability to the team.

A midseason trade proved critical to the team's success. GM Lou Gorman dealt for shortstop Spike Owen and outfielder Dave Henderson. Owen supplied some dependability to the middle of the infield, while Henderson deepened the outfield and introduced a lively voice to the clubhouse.

But by far the biggest change was a fully healthy Roger Clemens. A former first-round pick, Clemens had made his debut in 1984 and his arrival offered the hope that the Sox would have an honest-to-goodness ace as part of their rotation for years to come. But a rotator cuff injury midway through the 1985 season sidelined him. He underwent surgery to repair the issue, but his career was thought to be in jeopardy.

To say that fear was misplaced would be a massive understatement. Clemens returned with a flourish in 1986, winning his first 14 decisions and going undefeated until July. He would go on to win not only the Cy Young Award—becoming the first Red Sox pitcher to do so since Jim Lonborg nearly 20 seasons earlier—but also the American League MVP award.

The Sox had their strengths. They were fifth in the AL in runs scored and fourth in OPS, suggesting a particularly good offensive team. But Clemens was the separator. He started 33 games that season, and the Red Sox won all but six. Of those six losses, two were 1–0 defeats.

As a team, they finished 29 games over .500 (95–66); in games started by Clemens, they were 21 games over .500.

The Sox coasted to their first division title in 11 seasons and were 9.5 games ahead of second-place New York in the final week of the season before the Yanks swept a meaningless four-game series to close out the schedule, giving the appearance of a more competitive race when, in fact, the AL East crown had been long before decided.

In the ALCS, the Sox drew the California Angels. After beating up Clemens in a shocking Game 1 upset at Fenway, the Angels earned a split of the first two games, then took the next two games in Anaheim to establish a seemingly impenetrable 3–1 lead in the series.

Trailing 5–2 in the ninth and three outs away from having their season ended, the Sox got two two-run homers from Baylor and Henderson to go up by a run. The Angels, in turn, rallied for a run of their own in the home half, setting up the second straight extra-inning game of the series.

In the 11th, Henderson came through again, providing a tie-breaking bases-loaded sacrifice fly to put the Sox up by a run. The Angels went down in order in the bottom of the inning and never recovered. Though still ahead in the series, which now returned to Boston, the Angels, seemingly demoralized, lost the next two games by a combined score of 18–5 as the Sox claimed the pennant.

That set up an epic World Series meeting between the Sox and the *other* team from New York, the Mets.

In an era long before interleague play, the Sox had almost no history with New York's National League entry. In truth, the Sox and Mets might have had more in common than not. Like the Sox, the Mets were accustomed to finishing second to the Yankees.

While the Yankees had the history, the immortal players, and, at the time, 22 world championships, the Mets had to be content with their one title, a triumph so thoroughly unexpected that it was referred to as a "miracle."

In their first 24 years of existence, the Mets had finished with a losing record 17 times. They may have worn the royal blue of the Dodgers and the orange of the Giants—the two New York–based National League teams who deserted the city for California after the 1957 season, leaving New York as a one-team town for the next four years—but they were the misfit toy of the city, and for the first half-dozen years of their history were the very measure of ineptitude.

Not for nothing did their first manager, Casey Stengel, once ask in frustration, "Can't anybody here play this game?"

But like the Red Sox, the Mets in 1986 were buoyed by a young pitching savant. The Red Sox had Clemens and the Mets had Dwight Gooden, a fireballer barely out of his teens. Also like the Red Sox, the Mets had survived a grueling LCS to arrive at the World Series.

In defeating the Houston Astros, the Mets had experienced four games decided by one run. They won the Series in six games, but the final two lasted a combined 28 innings—the equivalent length of three games.

The Series opened at Shea Stadium, and the Sox shocked the Mets, winners of 108 games during the season, by taking each of the first two contests to take an early, commanding edge. Just two wins in the next five games would deliver the Red Sox their elusive championship.

But the Mets answered back by taking the next two at Fenway, evening the series. A Game 5 win at Fenway by the Sox, however, positioned Boston perfectly. Returning to Queens, the Sox would get two chances at the clincher.

There's something about Game 6 in Red Sox postseason lore. In 1975, the Carlton Fisk home run in the 12th inning concluded what many regard as the greatest World Series game of all time. In 2004, Game 6 of the ALCS would come to be known as the "Bloody Sock" game, with Curt Schilling, having undergone an experimental surgical procedure on his ankle, defeating the Yankees in Yankee Stadium.

But Game 6 of the 1986 World Series would become legendary for all the wrong reasons, at least as far as the Sox were concerned.

First, there was the removal of Clemens, who had limited the Mets to two runs over the first seven innings. But with Clemens due to hit in the top of the eighth, despite having thrown just 72 pitches to that point, McNamara inserted pinch-hitter Mike Greenwell to hit for his starter.

After the game, and for years to come, McNamara would insist that Clemens had asked out of the game.

"He came off the mound in the bottom of the [seventh] inning and we were waiting there at the steps," recalled McNamara decades later with the MLB Network, "to congratulate him you know, [on] getting out of the seventh and he came down the steps and he said, 'That's all I can pitch.' Quote, unquote."

McNamara added that a small cut on a finger on Clemens' pitching hand had begun to develop and that was the cause of his pitcher's self-proclaimed withdrawal.

Clemens has angrily disputed this recollection, insisting that he never asked out.

Predictably, the move unfolded disastrously for the Red Sox. Greenwell, a rookie, was overpowered and struck out. Then, in the bottom of the eighth, the Mets rallied to tie the game off reliever Calvin Schiraldi.

The game remained tied until the 10th, when Henderson—that man again—homered and Marty Barrett's RBI single scored another run. Now three outs from the clincher, the Sox led by two.

It then got better before it almost inevitably got worse. Much, much worse.

Schiraldi, working his third inning, retired the first two Mets he faced in the bottom of the inning. The Mets flashed a congratulatory message on the scoreboard, saluting the 1986 World Champion Boston Red Sox. Jean Yawkey, 10 years after her husband's passing, was escorted to the visitor's clubhouse so she could partake in the trophy presentation.

Meanwhile, a few Mets position players moved from the dugout to the clubhouse, convinced that their season was over.

Then, like a trickle, it began. A single, then another, then a third. One run in, the Boston lead shaved to a run. A pitching change resulted in Bob Stanley replacing Schiraldi, and soon, a wild pitch by Stanley, allowing another run to score and forging a tie game.

As Shea erupted in delirium, it was if the inning was serving as a microcosm of the Red Sox's tortured history. Suddenly, the game stopped resembling a taut World Series matchup and devolved into a manifestation of Murphy's Law.

The Red Sox had gone from being one strike away from finally winning it all, and now, everything was going wrong. The three singles. The wild pitch. And finally, the error by first baseman Bill Buckner on a routine grounder by Mookie Wilson, allowing the winning run to score.

MLB officials scrambled to remove the makeshift stage that had been constructed in the visitor's clubhouse. Red Sox players walked off the field and resembled zombies, unable to process what had transpired. Boggs sat among the din of the ballpark and sobbed in the visitor's dugout.

Screenwriters couldn't have scripted the improbable ending. Even a franchise accustomed to cruel endings could not have foreseen this one. No one could have.

The loss helped spur the theory that the Red Sox had not just been unlucky in their futile pursuit of a World Series win, but actually cursed, thanks to the franchise's ill-fated decision to trade off Babe Ruth, the most dominant player the game had ever known.

If McNamara thought removing Clemens in the eighth would dog him forever, he now had a new question to answer eternally: Why had he not replaced Buckner with Dave Stapleton, as he had done previously in the same postseason when the Sox led late in games?

For his part, Buckner would become, for some, the ultimate villain, the convenient whipping boy, the personification of the Red Sox's decades-long futility. (Eventually, Buckner would return to Fenway as a member of the Sox again in 1990 and be treated more warmly. But Buckner never fully got over the crazed bitterness that he was subjected to by some in the media and the team's fan base. Long before the appellation evolved into an acronym for the Greatest of All Time, Buckner was a "goat" of a different kind.)

In all the craziness, it was almost easy to forget that the Red Sox had only lost Game 6 and not the Series itself. There was still another game to be played, still another chance for them to win it and the championship.

Ominously, it rained the next night, forcing the postponement of the deciding Game 7. That should have been a sign. It also gave the Red Sox another 24 hours to contemplate what had unfolded in the bottom of the 10th, and that might not have served them well. A quicker return to action could have been a positive, enabling them to move forward more quickly.

But anyone who had seen Game 6 and was reasonably acquainted with Red Sox history knew how this would end. Not even a 3–0 Red Sox lead after five was enough to convince anyone otherwise. Sure enough, the Mets rallied for three runs in both the sixth and seventh, and not even two more Red Sox runs in the top of the eighth were enough to save the day.

As the final out was recorded in the ninth and the Sox's fate officially sealed, Mets reliever Jesse Orosco collapsed on the ground.

But it was the Red Sox who had been figuratively brought to their knees. The careers of Buckner, Stanley, and McNamara would, in some ways, never recover.

And for Red Sox fans, it would take almost two decades to expunge the nightmare from their consciousness.

PART 7

THE GOLDEN AGE

18

2004

When you go almost 90 years in between World Series championships, there has to be more to it than just bad luck.

Yes, it was the Red Sox's misfortune, for three straight trips to the Fall Classic—1967, 1975, and 1986—to play the National League champion with the best record of any NL pennant winner from that decade.

And yes, given that all three Series went a full seven games before the Red Sox lost each time, surely some bad breaks and debatable calls played parts.

Then there was the institutional racism, the startling inability to acknowledge the importance of pitching, and other factors.

But when the Sox finally, ultimately, at long last won the 2004 World Series, it became apparent that their long drought may have also had something to do with makeup.

The Red Sox, of course, had had great players before—several of whom are now represented in Cooperstown. They'd had capable managers; savvy front office executives; and, say what you will about him, a supportive, eager-to-spend longtime owner.

Not until 2004, however, did they have the proper *mix* of players, the right combination of personalities, the perfect alchemy to win it all.

The 2004 club had that because both Theo Epstein and Terry Francona intuitively understood that it took a special player to survive and thrive in Boston.

While there are other big-market, high-pressure cities—New York and Philadelphia immediately come to mind—Boston, pre-2004, was probably in a class by itself.

Every year that didn't end with a championship was a failure. A combustible media environment—egged on by talk shows that traded in recrimination and blame—and a loyal fan base starved by the long title drought helped to make Boston a challenge for many players.

Some players were mystified by the unending focus on past failures—the recountings of 1978 or 1986—and wondered what all of that had to do with them. Some didn't understand the linkage between past teams and their own. When a modern-day player committed an error, was it necessary to invoke the memory of Bill Buckner? Must a rookie pitcher be reminded of the travails of Bobby Sprowl, circa 1978?

Such references were, to the players, ancient history, unrelated to them. For the fans, however, it was all linear—a long, connective string of disappointments, one after another.

The fog of negativity that hung over the club—with some lingering from the previous October and Game 7 of the 2003 ALCS heartbreak at Yankee Stadium—wasn't going to be lifted anytime soon. It would linger until the Red Sox changed the narrative by finally winning.

If the 2003 season taught the front office anything—other than the need for a more reactive manager—it was that the team needed additional starting pitching. In Curt Schilling, the Red Sox found the perfect supplement to the rotation.

Only a few years earlier, Schilling had faced the Yankees in the 2001 World Series and emerged victorious, starting and besting Roger Clemens in Game 7.

Schilling had willingly embraced the challenge of defeating the game's most storied franchise. The Yankees already had the most championships in baseball history, and when the 9/11 attacks took place and the Yankees advanced to the World Series less than two months after that horrific event, it seemed that the baseball gods had arranged for New York to emerge victorious.

Prior to Game 1 of the 2001 World Series, with Schilling set to pitch for the Arizona Diamondbacks, I asked him about the task of combating the "mystique and aura" associated with MLB's most storied franchise.

"Those are dancers in a nightclub," Schilling said, dismissively. "Those are not things we concern ourselves with on the ball field."

Two years later, after a Thanksgiving Day visit from Theo Epstein and assistant GM Jed Hoyer, Schilling waived his no-trade agreement and became a member of the Sox.

He understood the expectations that came with such an assignment, and instead of shrinking from them, embraced them wholeheartedly.

Not long after Schilling was dealt to the Sox, he filmed a commercial for New England Ford Dealers. In it, Schilling was shown hitchhiking in the desert. He got into a truck with his Red Sox equipment bag and when the driver asked where he was headed, Schilling replied: "Boston—gotta break an 86-year-old curse."

His frankness and willingness to embrace the situation made Schilling an instant favorite of the fan base. Here was someone who spoke their language, who arrived with a healthy hatred of the rival Yankees.

Schilling's willingness to embrace chances to defeat the Evil Empire—as Red Sox CEO and president Larry Lucchino had humorously dubbed them—didn't end with his arrival into town.

That October, before starting in Game 1 of the 2004 ALCS at Yankee Stadium, Schilling understood his responsibility and relished the assignment.

"I'm not sure I can think of any scenario more enjoyable than making 55,000 people from New York shut up," said Schilling.

Here was someone, clearly, who didn't worry about providing additional motivation for the opponent or fret about providing bulletin board material. Schilling said what was on his mind—this would become more problematic in his post–playing career—and didn't apologize.

The Red Sox had others who were equally irreverent, who had just the proper kind of "don't back down" attitude.

Kevin Millar didn't have the career credentials to match those of Schilling. He had never been an All-Star, had never been a contender for an individual award, and certainly had never shared a World Series MVP trophy the way Schilling had.

But Millar had something that couldn't be voted upon or awarded. He had a carefree spirit, an easygoing way that allowed him to ignore the noise that could so easily envelop a Red Sox team.

It was Millar—part DH, part first baseman, part clubhouse clown—who came up with the phrase "Cowboy Up" for the Sox. It was Millar's rallying cry, a way to motivate his teammates.

In the middle of a losing streak? About to begin a big series? Ready to dive headlong into the postseason? It was time to "Cowboy Up."

It worked. If the Red Sox weren't exactly immune to the outside pressures and expectations associated with playing for the team, they could lower the volume by acting like kids whose parents had left them home for the weekend.

So, it wasn't unusual for Johnny Damon to be performing naked pullups in the home clubhouse at Fenway minutes before gametime.

Some of this atmosphere was the result of manager Terry Francona enforcing few rules and allowing the players to be themselves—however dangerous that might have sometimes been. But Francona trusted his players to get their work in and be prepared for games.

If they then stretched the boundaries of good taste or defied baseball convention, what was the harm?

Of course, it helped that even the team's star players were larger-than-life personalities who didn't shy away from expressing themselves.

Ace Pedro Martinez, when confronted with the specter of the Curse of the Bambino, issued a challenge to the slugger's ghost: "Wake up the damn Bambino, and I'll drill him in the ass!" exclaimed an exasperated Martinez.

Slugger David Ortiz, motivated to prove the Minnesota Twins had committed an epic miscalculation by releasing him after 2002, began to view every at-bat as an opportunity at redemption.

And then there was Manny Ramirez.

Ramirez wasn't new to the team, having signed a massive free agent deal with the Sox after the 2000 season. But with each passing year, the legendary tales of "Manny being Manny" grew more widespread.

Contrary to public perception, Ramirez was a student of hitting. He would typically arrive at the ballpark late in the morning or early in the afternoon to watch video of that night's opposing starting pitcher. He would take extra batting practice, hit flips in the cage, and work on his timing before leaving for a midday nap.

Ramirez's persona was that of a carefree swinger who got by on God-given talent and little else. But that was hardly the case. Ramirez worked at his craft and studiously prepared for his at-bats, treating each as a precious opportunity.

There were tales—apocryphal or not—of Ramirez intentionally missing pitches early in an at-bat in an effort to disarm the pitcher and induce him to throw the same pitch again, either later in the same at-bat or perhaps the next one. Then, Ramirez would be positioned to club the same pitch that he had awkwardly whiffed on earlier.

But Ramirez was not immune to some strange behavior, some of which his teammates found entertaining, and some they did not.

In Baltimore for a series against the Orioles during 2004, Damon raced back to track a ball hit by the Orioles' David Newhan. Finally retrieving the ball on the Camden Yards warning track, Damon, who was not blessed with a major league–caliber arm, turned to fling the ball back into the infield as quickly as he could.

Ramirez, who had sprinted over from left field to back up the play, lunged at Damon's weak offering—even though the ball had traveled only about 75 feet. It was then up to Ramirez to make yet another throw to the Red Sox infielder stationed on the lip of the infield. The additional exchange on the unexpected cutoff meant that what should have been a triple for Newhan was, instead, an inside-the-park home run.

In other words, this was not a group burdened by pressures. They were too busy enjoying themselves.

Sometimes, improving clubhouse chemistry came as a result of subtraction rather than addition.

When Epstein determined that the Sox needed a mid-season shakeup—both to improve a subpar infield defense and to bolster the team's delicate clubhouse chemistry—he gambled on unloading Nomar Garciaparra.

Garciaparra, who had two batting titles earlier in his career, had become a liability in the infield. Of equal concern was that he had become a sullen presence in the clubhouse, alternately railing at ownership for withdrawing an earlier contract extension and at the local media for what he perceived to be their suffocating and unnecessarily—in his mind, anyway—negative coverage.

He had a line added to the carpet in the home clubhouse, to keep reporters away from his locker. He bitterly complained about scoring decisions and in general, seemed to be brooding about some perceived slight or another.

When Garciaparra was shipped out in a complicated four-team deal at the deadline, it was as though a fog had been lifted in the clubhouse. No more conspiracy theories or complaints about the local media being out to get the Sox.

In Garciaparra's place came shortstop Orlando Cabrera, who played with a light spirit and infectious energy. He soon was a crowd favorite.

Still, for all the transformations to the team's makeup, they found themselves just nine innings away from being swept in the American League Championship, capped by a 19–8 shellacking in Game 3.

After all that had been done to improve over last year—the trade for Schilling; the signing of Keith Foulke; the trade-deadline blockbuster—were the Sox really going to go down in such ignominious fashion? A year prior, they had at least fought and scrapped to go seven games—and into extra innings at that—before losing. Now, were they really going to be swept, in front of their own fans?

In the owners' suite, John Henry, Tom Werner, and Larry Lucchino crafted a press release congratulating the Yankees on their victory. It had come to this.

Or had it?

Trailing by a run and down to their final three outs, the Red Sox stirred. A walk by Millar, followed by a stolen base by pinch-runner Dave Roberts, and then a run-scoring single from Bill Mueller, tied the score and sent Fenway into a fever pitch.

It guaranteed them nothing except extra innings, but suddenly there was life for the Sox.

But what seemed like a face-saving rally, ensuring that they wouldn't be embarrassed by a sweep—at least not one in nine innings' time—turned out to be something far larger. It was, in fact, the beginning of the greatest comeback effort in baseball history.

Never had a team trailing three games to none come back to win a best-of-seven postseason series.

But from the time Roberts crossed the plate with the tying run, the momentum began to shift, and with it came a seismic realignment of the two team's shared histories. From that point on, the Red Sox dominated.

They won Game 4 in extra innings, then did the same in Game 5 the next night, needing 14 innings to extend the series further. That moved the ALCS back to New York, but not even regaining home field advantage could reverse the Yankees' plight. The Sox, behind a herculean effort from Schilling, took Game 6, too, setting up, for the second straight October, a winner-take-all Game 7 in the Bronx.

This one, however, was nothing like the previous one. The Sox scored two in the first and four more in the second, draining the drama out of Yankee Stadium. For a change, destiny seemed to have taken a seat in the Boston dugout.

A year earlier, I had entered the visitor's clubhouse at Yankee Stadium after Game 7, where the lone sound came from grown men quietly sobbing into their lockers. But on this night, a party had erupted, with champagne flowing and players jumping for joy, and, perhaps, in a demonstration of relief.

Pedro Martinez emerged from a back room with the American League Championship trophy in his arms, burst into the center of the mad celebration, thrust it skyward, and exclaimed: "Look what I found!"

The World Series that followed was less of a Fall Classic and more of a *fait accompli*. The Red Sox steamrolled over the St. Louis Cardinals in the first three games, and prior to Game 4, Terry Francona sat in his office at Busch Stadium, seemingly without a care in the world.

Francona, like most baseball lifers, was prone to superstition, and the last thing he wanted to do was to take a world championship for granted. But mostly, he was being polite and respectful to his opponents. He had watched his team win their last seven games in a row, and the Cardinals looked for all the world like a team whose will had been broken.

For all their tortured history, for all the cruel wins snatched from their grasp over the decades, this Red Sox team would not—*could* not—be denied.

19

2007

The Red Sox had spared no expense en route to their first championship in 86 years.

Their payroll that season was second highest in the game that season—behind only the New York Yankees, naturally—and for the next few seasons that followed.

A look at the core group from 2004 revealed that many of the most important figures on that roster were either free agents (Manny Ramirez, Keith Foulke, Johnny Damon), or trade acquisitions (Curt Schilling, Pedro Martinez) obtained from small-market teams in search of salary relief.

It was a star-studded group, full of outsize personalities.

There were other key contributors on the roster who were castoffs from elsewhere, including Kevin Millar and David Ortiz. There were midseason acquisitions such as Doug Mientkiewicz and Orlando Cabrera and Dave Roberts, and more modest free-agent signings like Mike Timlin and Bill Mueller.

Even players who had been with the organization for several years—Tim Wakefield, Jason Varitek, and Derek Lowe among them—had originally come over via trade.

That 2004 team was a mixed bag, then, of castoffs, free-agent superstars, complementary players, and journeymen, all combining to deliver Boston its long-awaited title.

What the 2004 team didn't have, however, were many homegrown players.

In fact, on the 2004 postseason roster, the lone player drafted or signed and then developed by the Red Sox was Trot Nixon.

That's it.

One.

Every other player on that roster began his professional career elsewhere before landing with the Sox, either having been released, or signed as a free agent, or acquired in a trade.

That assemblage was testament to the work of Theo Epstein, and prior to him, Dan Duquette, along with countless scouts who had made recommendations, filed reports, and seen their advice heeded. Each deserved credit for the finished product that wrote itself into baseball history and the hearts of New England sports fans.

It was a unique mix, to be sure, but Epstein understood something else, too. Such a plan was not sustainable.

Even though the Sox hit it big with Ramirez, Foulke, and Damon, deals they would do again in a heartbeat, free agency was, at best, inefficient and, at worst, a potentially disastrous allocation of resources.

The Red Sox were fortunate that they had enough resources to overcome the occasional misstep in free agency. So, when Edgar Renteria proved to be a huge mistake in the team's search for a more long-term solution at shortstop, the Sox simply moved on from him and focused elsewhere.

(Small-market teams had no such luxury, forced to live with the consequences of their own miscalculations until such time as the contract expired, or they could convince a more well-heeled competitor to take an underperforming player off their hands.)

The Sox had gotten extraordinarily lucky with their own forays into free agency. Ramirez, for all his odd behavior and unpredictability, proved to be a run-producing machine and was arguably the best righthanded hitter in the game during his tenure in Boston.

Damon and Foulke, meanwhile, performed heroically even if they never again reached the heights they attained in 2004.

But Epstein fully understood that overspending for talent on the open market each winter would eventually become a losing proposition. For one thing, it would lead to permanently overstuffed payrolls. For another, just because the Red Sox had enjoyed fabulous results in free agency was no guarantee that that trend would continue.

When the Red Sox imploded in the summer of 2006, dropping out of playoff contention, it was a direct reminder to Epstein that it was time to overhaul the roster again.

In 2003 and 2004, the team had aimed high and spent big, in part because the Henry-Werner-Lucchino ownership troika wanted to convince the fan base that, despite being labeled by some as "carpetbaggers," they were fully committed to putting a winning product on the field and weren't afraid to spend in an effort to demonstrate that.

But with two trips to the ALCS, three consecutive trips to the postseason—for the first time in franchise history—and, of course, a World Champions pennant flying over Fenway, they had made their point.

Now, it was time to shift gears.

When Epstein was hired after the 2002 season, he vowed to turn the Red Sox into a "scouting and player development machine."

For his first few seasons in charge, that plan seemed to be put on hold as he assembled a more veteran roster, one capable of winning *now*. With that accomplished and the major league roster getting older and players aging out of their prime, Epstein saw that it was time to change his approach.

In the immediate aftermath of 2004, Epstein had begun to cut ties with that championship roster. Of the four free-agents-to-be from that magical team—Pedro Martinez, Derek Lowe, Orlando Cabrera, and Jason Varitek—Epstein retained just one: Varitek.

They were not altogether popular moves. Martinez was adored by the fan base for his brilliance on the mound and his charisma. Lowe, who began the postseason in the team's doghouse after a poor September, managed to be the winning pitcher in the final game of all three postseason series. And Cabrera, though a short-timer, was quickly welcomed by the fans.

But Epstein knew that the Sox, even with their resources, had to pick and choose. Not every veteran player could be retained. More to the point, not every veteran player *should* be retained. Doing so could be counterproductive in more ways than one: first, it would lead to permanent payroll inflation. Second, it would block the migration of prospects from the team's minor league system.

In the short term, Epstein had to deal with diminishing returns. Two starting pitchers, signed to short-term deals and brought on board to replace the holes created by the departure of Martinez and Lowe, flopped—David Wells and Matt Clement.

But those were mere placeholders for the Sox. In the long term, Epstein was looking for internal solutions.

He found two in Jacoby Ellsbury and Clay Buchholz. The irony is that both were initially drafted as compensation picks for losing Martinez and Lowe.

Ellsbury made his debut late in 2007 and before long was a lineup staple. Buchholz tossed a no-hitter in his second major league start and, while he wasn't part of the 2007 postseason roster, was a fixture in the rotation for the next nine seasons.

Two other key contributors in 2007 were Dustin Pedroia and Jonathan Papelbon—also homegrown.

Pedroia made his debut the previous season and appeared to be overmatched. Undersized but hyperconfident, he swung with abandon and played with a permanent chip on his shoulder.

In the opening weeks of the 2007 season, Pedroia looked no more ready to compete at the big-league level, striking out at an alarming rate. His early failure seemed to confirm the skepticism many in the game had when the Sox selected him out of Arizona State with their first pick in the 2004 draft.

But by mid-May, Pedroia had stabilized, stolen the second base job from veteran Alex Cora, and emerged as a linchpin in the Boston lineup. Over time, once his play matched his outsize personality, his cocksure nature became a little easier to tolerate.

That October, Pedroia would ignite the Red Sox by homering off Colorado's Jeff Francis leading off the first inning of Game 1 of the 2007 World Series, setting the tone for the remainder of the games. Days later, when a suspicious Coors Field security guard at the players' entrance had to be convinced that Pedroia was indeed a member of the Sox—Pedroia had forgotten to bring his player ID—Pedroia strutted into the ballpark in a huff, then turned around to chastise the guard one last time.

"Why don't you ask Jeff Fucking Francis who the fuck I am?" bellowed Pedroia. "I'm the guy who hit a bomb and just ended their fucking season."

If Pedroia was full of bravado, Papelbon was the latest in a long line of rebel pitchers.

Papelbon seemed like a character from another era. He would have fit in nicely with the Red Sox's legendary Buffalo Heads—a group of irreverent pitchers in the late 1970s, led by Bill Lee, who seemed to exist just to torture old school manager Don Zimmer.

Papelbon was, well, *different.*

Different enough that he bet teammate Kevin Youkilis he could start a season with 10 scoreless innings, or, as punishment, sculpt his hair into a mohawk cut. Sure enough, Papelbon hit the 10-inning mark without allowing a run, then decided to go for the mohawk anyway—because he liked the look.

Different enough that, in an homage to NFL star Chad Johnson, who legally changed his last name to "Ochocinco" to reflect his uniform number 85, Papelbon began referring to himself as "Cinco Ocho"—in reference to his own uniform number 58.

In football, it's often placekickers who have quirky personalities; in hockey, it's the goaltenders. And in baseball, the unusual characters often reside in the bullpen. Think: Sparky Lyle, Al Hrabosky, and, of course, Papelbon.

To be sure, opposing hitters found little comic relief stepping into the box against Papelbon. He combined a heavy four-seam fastball with a devastating slider and splitter to befuddle hitters. In a four-year stretch, from 2006 through 2009, Papelbon converted 151 saves—an average of nearly 38 per season—while posting a 1.74 ERA and a WHIP of 0.917.

Papelbon was at the height of his dominance in 2007 when he tossed 10.2 scoreless innings and executed a brilliant pickoff of Rockies outfielder Matt Holliday in the eighth inning of a one-run Game 2 of the World Series, effectively snuffing out Colorado's hopes to take the Series.

And, of course, there is the image, frozen in the minds of Red Sox fans of a certain age, of Papelbon, having recorded the final out of the '07 Series in Denver, with arms outstretched toward the plate, beckoning a celebratory leap from Varitek.

Later, Papelbon none-too-artfully danced an Irish jig in the postgame celebration. He delivered an encore performance during the team's Duck Boat parade around Boston days later.

Not all the newbies contributed significantly right away.

Jon Lester, who would go to be a mainstay in the rotation, win 110 games for the Sox and develop into a workhorse, pitching 200 or more innings five times in the span of six seasons, spent part of the year rehabbing from leukemia. But Lester also returned in time to start and win the clinching game of the World Series that October.

Finally, there was Ellsbury, whose athleticism and speed allowed him to supplant Coco Crisp as the team's starting center fielder. Ellsbury emerged as a force in the postseason, averaging a run scored and a double per game while making several circus catches in the outfield. He reached base in half of his plate appearances and became a threat to steal every time he did.

In the years to come, Ellsbury would frustrate the Red Sox to no end with his fragility. But when healthy, he was a dynamic figure, capable of disrupting opposing teams and using his speed to cover huge swaths of the Fenway lawn.

The 2007 championship couldn't help but seem somewhat anticlimactic after the first. It could never match the 2004 title, which served to cleanse all of New England as the most iconic triumph in franchise history.

But in its own way, it was unique. This was the Red Sox's chance to prove that they weren't buying a championship and that they weren't dependent on free agents or inheriting players from a previous management group.

In that sense, it reflected positively on the organization, from top to bottom—not just Epstein and his band of young, whip-smart assistants, but also the team's amateur scouts, its minor league coaches and managers and field coordinators. They also had a hand in what resulted in the 2007 championship.

In that sense, it was as—if not more—rewarding for all involved, and a reminder that there was more than one way to assemble a great major league roster.

The fact was that, despite Epstein's hopes, this "scouting and player development machine" did not produce any sort of mini-dynasty. The team returned to the ALCS the following year but lost out in an epic seven-game set to the upstart Rays.

After that, the organization began a slow free fall. They would get swept out of the Division Series in 2009, miss the postseason altogether in 2010 and 2011—leading to the exit of both Francona and Epstein—and finally, bottom out with a sharp plummet into the basement in 2012.

In later years, the team would deviate from the lesson of 2007 and attempt quick fixes through expensive forays into free agency.

But 2007 stood as evidence that, just as the Red Sox had learned to blend advanced analytics with more traditional scouting to best evaluate players, an organization would be well-served to understand that the best way to enjoy sustained contention was to build a foundation of homegrown players.

20

2013

To fully appreciate the Red Sox's third championship in the span of 10 seasons, the team that won in 2013, you first must understand where they were coming from.

The 2012 season was an unmitigated disaster, from start to finish.

Against all logic, the team had inexplicably hired Bobby Valentine as its manager. Valentine hadn't managed in the big leagues in the past decade and in his first 15 seasons had taken his team to the playoffs only twice.

But team president Larry Lucchino, fearful that the Red Sox clubhouse had become directionless in the final season under Terry Francona, determined that Valentine would be the perfect tonic.

Valentine wasted no time alienating players when he embarrassed veteran infielder Mike Aviles during a spring training drill. A few weeks into the season, he publicly questioned the desire of Kevin Youkilis. And it was all downhill from there.

Hopelessly out of contention in the second half, the Sox sold off a trio of veterans—Carl Crawford, Josh Beckett, and Adrian Gonzalez—to the Los Angeles Dodgers, and the team sputtered to the finish line, finishing with a losing record for the first time in 15 years.

The day after the season, the team moved swiftly to relieve Valentine of his duties, in the hopes that his brief but disastrous tenure would soon be forgotten, like a political leader who had fallen out of favor, never to be heard from again.

In Valentine's place, the team turned to John Farrell, whom it had tried, unsuccessfully, to hire the previous winter. Farrell, who had managed the Toronto Blue Jays in each of the previous two seasons, had been the Sox pitching coach from 2007 to 2010.

The move was hugely popular with the players, especially the pitchers who had worked under Farrell in his first stint with the club. There was a lightness around the team that had been absent the previous season, and given the team's pitching woes, Farrell's return spurred optimism.

But an incident in the first month came to serve as the defining moment of the season.

An hour or so following the team's traditional Patriots' Day game at Fenway, two explosions set off by terrorists near the finish line of the annual running of the Boston Marathon resulted in four fatalities and sent shockwaves through the entire region.

The Red Sox were on their team bus, headed for Logan Airport and the start of a brief, one-city road trip to Cleveland, when players and staff members began hearing of the tragedy.

The next night, as all of New England dealt with the aftershocks, the Red Sox tried to make sense of it all. Clubhouse manager Tommy McLaughlin, with some input from outfielder Jonny Gomes, hung a jersey in the visitors' dugout in Cleveland, with BOSTON STRONG stitched across the back.

It would become the rallying cry for the city, the commonwealth, and, by extension, the team.

The three games in Cleveland may as well have been played on Mars. Though the Sox were just over 600 miles from their hometown, they felt as though they were on the other side of the world.

Back in Boston, families of the players had to deal with the immediate aftershocks. Boston was gripped by confusion, uncertainty, and fear as at least one of the bombers remained on the loose. The greater Boston area was under a shelter in place order as a manhunt ensued to find the perpetrator.

The Sox were scheduled to begin a homestand on Friday, April 12, but that was postponed as the search continued. When the last suspect was apprehended, the Sox were given the go-ahead to resume play at Fenway.

What transpired the following day—prior to the game, and then during—will long live in the memories of anyone who experienced it.

In an emotional, unscripted address, David Ortiz, who had spent Patriots' Day at the team's Triple A affiliate in Pawtucket, Rhode Island, rehabbing an Achilles injury, spoke for his teammates and, by extension, all of New England.

"This," thundered Ortiz into a microphone, "is our fucking city. And we're not going to let anyone dictate our freedoms."

It was if Ortiz had struck a responsive chord. In plain—if profane—language, unscripted, and reacting with a mixture of outrage, defiance, and pride, this adopted son of the Dominican

Republic, who had become a U.S. citizen only five years earlier, served to unite a region.

Throughout the season, the Sox's commitment to the cause was unceasing. Players visited victims of the bombing in local hospitals while the team held ceremonies to honor law enforcement and first responders who had selflessly sought out the perpetrators while tending to the injured.

The response was genuine, and though it was undertaken with a genuine and altruistic intent, the commitment shown by the Red Sox had an unintended consequence.

Starting in 2011, when reports leaked of players spending time in the clubhouse drinking beer and eating fried chicken—*during games*—and continuing the following year under the clownish presence of Valentine, the goodwill generated by the two world championships and near-regular presence in the playoffs had dissipated.

Suddenly, the notion of the Red Sox ending the curse and becoming one of baseball's most dominant franchises seemed like a long time ago. The Patriots had begun a dynasty of their own. The Celtics had made a return to glory—however briefly—with a 2008 championship and a rallying cry from Kevin Garnett that "anything is possible!" The Bruins had won one Stanley Cup (2011) and narrowly lost a second two years later.

In 2013, after four straight years out of the playoffs, the Red Sox's popularity began to ebb. Television ratings flatlined, and a Fenway Park sellout streak 10 years in the making ended.

But in the aftermath of the team's heartfelt response to the Marathon bombing, the players seemed more real, more human. The perception of the club as an uncaring collection of millionaires, gorging themselves on booze and fast food, was changed.

Putting aside the catastrophe of Patriots' Day and the bonding that emanated from it, the 2013 Red Sox were a collection of castoffs.

In the previous winter, GM Ben Cherington, about to enter his second year in that post, scoured the free agent market to help piece together his roster.

There were holdovers—Ortiz, Dustin Pedroia, Jacoby Ellsbury, Jon Lester, John Lackey—and there were players making the transition to the big leagues—Will Middlebrooks, Jackie Bradley Jr. But more was needed.

So, Cherington opted for several short-term deals for free agents who were looking for make-good opportunities. Some were coming off injuries; others had just weathered down years. Cherington divided up his offseason dollars, and rather than make one dramatic signing, he spread out his allocated resources.

Among his gambles: outfielders Jonny Gomes and Shane Victorino, first baseman Mike Napoli, catcher David Ross, and starting pitcher Ryan Dempster.

All five had something to prove, and all five had something else in common: they were strong clubhouse personalities.

The Red Sox did not exactly lack for leadership. After all, any team that already included Pedroia and Ortiz was not going to be a passive one.

But as an organization, the Red Sox had been through a lot in the previous two years. The 2011 team had squandered a sizable lead for the wild-card spot in September and were eliminated in the final inning of the final game of the season, leading, indirectly, to the departure of both manager Terry Francona and Theo Epstein.

After becoming the first team in the 21st century to capture two World Series, the Red Sox had grown dysfunctional.

The following year, the team endured a miserable season under the tutelage of Valentine, whose brusque ways helped to alienate nearly everyone.

Clearly, some stability was necessary, and Cherington kept that in mind when he pieced together his team. Gomes and Victorino were high-energy types who provided spark. Napoli was quieter, but intense. Dempster offered veteran know-how and comic relief—his impressions were side-splitting—and Ross, as befits a veteran catcher, had an innate sense of leadership. It was no surprise that, several years later, he became a major league manager, without having managed a game at any other level.

Those handful of players served as liaison between the rest of the roster and Farrell. Managing in Boston is demanding enough—what with the many media responsibilities and having to serve as the public face of the franchise—without having to put out any smoldering fires in the clubhouse.

It's not always easy for newcomers to assert themselves on a team. They must be conscious of not usurping the roles of the existing veteran players and not alienate others.

But Gomes, Victorino, Napoli, Ross, and Dempster understood where that line was drawn.

It probably wasn't an accident that the newcomers all took part in a trend begun in spring training by Gomes, who grew out a beard that looked like it was inspired by the Smith Brothers featured on a box of cough drops.

In the late 1960s, when iconoclasts like Joe Namath and Derek Sanderson began wearing their hair long and growing facial hair, it was seen as an act of rebellion. Quaint as it might seem now, the idea of long hair was something of a political statement. These athletes weren't about to conform, nor were they going to worry about expressing their own style.

In 2013, hair length and beards no longer qualified as a particularly revolutionary statement. Rather, the sudden preponderance of beards signaled that this was a unified group, with the beards signaling membership in their own private club.

Meanwhile, a trade-deadline acquisition brought the Red Sox another veteran presence, to say nothing of the rotation depth that Jake Peavy provided. In one of his first outings for the team, he reacted incredulously to the sight of manager John Farrell emerging from the dugout to remove him from a start in which he allowed one run into the sixth inning.

TV cameras caught Peavy saying, "You've got to be fucking kidding me" as Farrell emerged, and the exchange on the mound, with the pitcher handing over the ball to the manager, was an awkward one. But Farrell correctly saw a veteran pitcher displaying his competitive streak and didn't take offense.

Emerging as a star in the second half was closer Koji Uehara. A journeyman Japanese reliever, he did not grow into the team's ninth-inning option until it had already first cycled through a handful of other options.

Uehara would enter games from the bullpen soundtracked by "Sandstorm," a bit of electronica that would not have sounded out of place in a Tokyo disco in the 1990s. Uehara could appear stoic on the mound, pounding his split-finger fastball into the strike zone with remarkable efficiency until he had secured the 27th out, at which point he took on the personality of a child arriving at his own surprise party, delighted by the surroundings.

Uehara would offer emphatic high fives to anyone in his path and sometimes found himself playfully thrown across the broad shoulders of Ortiz, who would truck him across the infield in celebration.

Coasting to a relatively easy division title, the Red Sox dispatched the Tampa Bay Rays without incident in the division series before tackling the Detroit Tigers in the ALCS.

The Sox had dropped Game 1 of the series and as they headed for the bottom of the eighth inning in Game 2 trailing 5–1, they had managed exactly one run in the first 16 innings.

Ortiz saved them, cranking a grand slam into the home bullpen in right, with Detroit outfielder Torii Hunter backpedaling in pursuit of the ball and falling over the bullpen wall, headfirst. The homer tied the game and indisputably changed the tenor of the series.

The Sox rallied for a walk-off win in the ninth and then took three of the next four to capture the pennant.

The 2013 World Series once more had the distinction of being anticlimactic.

After all the Red Sox had been through—from their third manager in as many years, to an influx of newcomers, to, of course, the Marathon bombing—it seemed inconceivable that they had journeyed this far to come up short.

And so, they didn't. There were a few uneasy moments in St. Louis, including the Sox suffering a crushing walk-off loss in Game 3, giving the Cardinals a 2–1 advantage.

But true to the spirit they had shown all season, the Sox were undeterred and ripped off three straight—the next two in St. Louis and the third back at Fenway.

Of the four World Series championships won by the Red Sox in the 21st century, this was the only one to be clinched at home. After all that had transpired just a few miles from the ballpark months earlier, and the special link that had grown between the city and the team, that only seemed fitting.

With one out in the top of the ninth in Game 6 and the Red Sox comfortably ahead 6–1, John Farrell allowed himself to say the quiet part out loud.

Leaning over to bench coach Torey Lovullo in the home dugout, with a sellout crowd roaring in anticipation, Farrell shouted above the din to be heard.

"Can you believe," asked Farrell, "we're about to win the World Series?"

It was, indeed, a difficult concept to grasp and one that would have seemed outlandish months earlier.

Three days later, as the Sox undertook the now familiar Duck Boat parade to celebrate yet another championship, the participants stopped at the Marathon finish line on Boylston Street, where back in April, tragedy struck, lives were lost, and somehow, a team came together.

21

2018

THE WONDER OF THE 2018 CHAMPIONSHIP SEASON, IN retrospect, wasn't that it came under the direction of a first-time manager.

While it is true that Alex Cora had never managed at any level—other than winter ball—before being hired by the Red Sox, Cora's leadership credentials and baseball acumen were unquestioned.

Nor was it terribly surprising that the Sox were able to build on the success they had had in the previous two seasons, when they won the American League East title each time, only to be derailed in the first round of the playoffs. In that sense, 2018 was simply a natural extension, the next logical milestone.

No, the biggest surprise was how (relatively) easy the whole thing seemed.

The Red Sox took over first place in the division on the fourth day of the season and remained there for the first five weeks. On June 26, they fell a half-game out of first for a day. On July 1, they were tied atop the division but, from that day onward, never so much as shared first. They led, day after day, over the final three months.

Their "low" point of the season came on June 21, when they were two full games behind the leader.

By the end, they won the division comfortably. Of the 185 days in the 2018 season, the Red Sox were either alone in first or owned a share of first in 173 of them.

The postseason was merely an extension of their regular season dominance. They trailed in their three series just once, after dropping the opener of the ALCS at home to the Houston Astros.

In the best-of-five division series, they trampled the New York Yankees with relative ease in five games. In the ALCS, after the Astros rabbit-punched them in Game 1, they won the next four in a row, including three straight in Houston, avenging an embarrassing loss in the division series the year before. And finally, they dusted the Los Angeles Dodgers in five games in the World Series; in the one game they lost, it took 18 innings to beat them.

They dominated from April through the end of October. They took on and beat all comers. They handily defeated three teams in the postseason, two of which had won 100 or more games during the season. They were never seriously threatened.

And that, ultimately, is the legacy of the 2018 Red Sox: they not only won, but they did so with ease. So much ease, in fact, that it was enough for Red Sox fans to wonder: Why did winning seem *so* hard for *so* long?

There were lessons from each of the other 21st century titles. In 2004, it was obvious that some personalities were better suited for Boston than others; in 2007, it was that the best way to build a sustainable roster was to largely rely on developing your own players; in 2013, we understood how external forces—and even tragedy—can create a bond that can't be broken.

As for 2018? Perhaps it helped that the organization had created something of a winning culture, with three titles in the previous 14 seasons. But at the end, as the Red Sox celebrated on the Dodger Stadium lawn, the overriding sensation was how simple it had seemed.

When the Red Sox made a personnel move, it worked.

When they needed a win, they almost always got one. (They never lost more than three games in a row all season.)

They won a franchise-record 108 games during the regular season, then lost just three times in the span of an almost month-long postseason.

Easy.

* * *

After the Red Sox dismissed John Farrell in October 2017, there seemed little doubt as to who his successor would be.

Cora had spent parts of four seasons as a player with the Red Sox, from 2005 through 2008, and was a member of the 2007 championship team. He knew, firsthand, the challenges of playing in Boston and was undeterred.

Like many successful managers, Cora wasn't a star in his playing days. Of his 14 seasons in the major leagues, just five of them saw him take part in 100 or more games. But he had grown up in a baseball family—his father played in Puerto Rico, then helped organize many of the island's youth leagues, while his older brother Joey, 10 years his senior, was an established big leaguer before Alex reached high school.

"I come from a country where they live baseball 24/7," Cora said. "In my family, for breakfast, we talk baseball. For lunch, we talk baseball, And for dinner, too."

In that sense, Cora was the perfect match for Boston, where the fabric of the game is stretched across generations, where fathers and grandfathers take their sons and grandsons to their first game, where the game is shared and enjoyed, like a family heirloom.

If Cora was a relative newcomer to the business of managing, his boss, president of baseball operations Dave Dombrowski, was an old hand.

After stints as a GM in Montreal, Miami, and Detroit, Dombrowski had been brought onboard by ownership in August 2015. It was an awkward transition, with Dombrowski hired to supplant GM Ben Cherington. Cherington, an acolyte of Theo Epstein, had done a masterful job in continuing the team's track record of developing young talent, but after 2013, the team's wildly unpredictable swings in on-field performance (last-place finishes in 2014 and 2015) began to reflect poorly upon him.

Ownership was getting antsy about the team's mercurial standing (three trips to the division basement in the span of four years) and decided it was time to turn to someone who had a track record of delivering in a hurry.

Sure enough, Dombrowski arrived with a clear win-now edict. All that stockpiling of all that talent had not resulted in much actual success, and Dombrowski was never known for his patience. In his previous stops—especially in Detroit—Dombrowski had operated on a mandate to produce a World Series contender, without much concern for the long-term impact.

Almost immediately, Dombrowski had gone to work. He traded for the closer (Craig Kimbrel) they lacked, signed one front-line starter (David Price), and then acquired another (Chris Sale).

Those three impact pitchers paid immediate dividends, leading to a couple of first-place finishes. But early exits in October on both occasions told Dombrowski there was more work to be done. So, in the winter of 2018, Dombrowski signed free-agent slugger J.D. Martinez.

Martinez sat on the open market all winter, available for the taking. Dombrowski seemed to slow-play the negotiations with super-agent Scott Boras. No other team made a meaningful multiyear offer, and a couple of weeks into the start of exhibition games, Martinez was in the fold.

He turned out to be, in some ways, the missing link, adding one more powerful bat to the middle of the Red Sox lineup. Prior to Martinez's arrival, the Red Sox had been decidedly lefthanded, with four regulars lefthanded and another platoon player (catcher Sandy Leon) a switch-hitter.

Martinez posted a 1.031 OPS and his .629 slugging percentage was further testament to his ability to mash. But Martinez was far, far more than a one-dimensional grip-it-and-rip-it power hitter. Martinez was a hitting savant who had rescued his own failing career after getting released by the Astros a half-dozen years earlier.

With the help of some private hitting instructors, with whom he worked tirelessly in-season and off, Martinez had remade himself by watching video, studying his own mechanics, and employing every bit of technology available. He had clubhouse attendants set up an iPad at the side of the batting cage, the better to analyze every single swing he took, whether it was in an otherwise empty cage early in the morning or on the back fields when he wasn't taking part in a game.

When Martinez wasn't immersed in video study or taking swings to fix a hitch in his swing, he was talking hitting—constantly. He served as a de facto third hitting coach, offering advice to teammates, providing counsel to younger players, and generally keeping the dugout conversation locked on hitting.

His impact was contagious. Teammate after teammate would credit him with spotting a defect or recognizing the smallest problem, be it a dropped front shoulder or a collapsed back leg. Even with a $23 million salary, Martinez was a bargain—not only for his in-game production, but for his impact on so many others.

The 2018 season also saw the blossoming of Mookie Betts.

Betts had had a breakout season in 2016, leading the American League in total bases while leading the team in both homers and RBI. But the 2018 season saw him graduate to the next level, in part because of the role that Cora had envisioned for him.

While serving as the bench coach in Houston in 2017, Cora had seen firsthand the impact a dynamic leadoff hitter could have. George Springer could drive the ball all over the ballpark, hit it out, and run the bases with abandon—the perfect blend of new-school leadoff man.

Cora saw the same qualities in Betts. He loved the idea that Betts was capable of giving the Sox a 1–0 lead one batter into the game, and the outfielder's blend of discipline (81 walks) and aggression proved to be the perfect tone-setter for the top of the Boston lineup.

But his offensive numbers only told one-third of the story. On the bases, Betts succeeded in stealing 30 bases in 36 tries, and he was awarded a Gold Glove for his play in right field, where he was credited with 19 defensive runs saved over the course of the season.

How dominant was Betts in that magical season of 2018? His WAR (Wins Above Replacement) was the third highest in franchise history and best since Carl Yastrzemski's magical Triple Crown season of 1967. In fact, since 1900, only 11 position players ever compiled a higher single-season WAR total than did Betts—and each is a Hall of Famer.

When he was hired, Cora preached the value of hunting fastballs, and in general, exhorted his players to go to the plate with the attitude of "Do Damage."

The Sox followed his lead. In 2018, they led the majors in the following categories: on-base percentage, total bases, hits, doubles, slugging percentage, and OPS. They also led all 30 teams in the single most important category—runs scored. And they did it all without succumbing to the all-or-nothing approach that was becoming commonplace in the game. While every other team was racking up record strikeout totals, the Sox were 25th in that category, demonstrating the ability to regularly put the ball in play.

In midseason, Dombrowski made several deals. In a seemingly minor transaction, he acquired Steve Pearce from Toronto to help improve the team's offense against lefthanded pitchers. No one—Dombrowski and Pearce included—could have foreseen how meaningful that small deal would become in October, when Pearce was named Most Valuable Player of the 2018 World Series.

The other big in-season acquisition was pitcher Nate Eovaldi, who provided additional rotation depth—especially critical when Chris Sale went down with a shoulder injury late in the season. In the postseason, Eovaldi proved his value by contributing both to the rotation (two starts) and the bullpen (four appearances, including a marathon six-inning stint that was both record-breaking and staff-saving).

Cora distinguished himself further in the postseason when he utilized a novel managerial approach. He used starters like Eovaldi for one-inning relief stints, deepening his staff. Rather than having them throw side sessions to keep sharp between starting assignments, Cora called on starters to contribute from the bullpen.

Such a strategy accomplished a few things. First, it added a layer of unpredictability to the team's pitching plans. The opposition could no longer focus on a couple of high-leverage relievers in their late-inning preparation since they were now unsure of whom they would face. Secondly, it improved the entire team's feeling of usefulness, knowing that literally any player could contribute on a given day. Finally, it helped to cover up a perceived weakness at the back end of the bullpen, especially with Kimbrel struggling with his control.

When it came time to close out the Series in Game 5 at Dodger Stadium, Cora again strayed from orthodoxy and called on Sale—and not Kimbrel—to secure the final three outs. Sale did so with style, fanning L.A.'s Manny Machado, who lunged on one knee at an unhittable slider.

It was the perfect ending to a near-perfect season. Never had a Red Sox team won more games in the regular season. Never had one played so many postseason games (14) and lost so few.

The identity of the opponents was not without note. First, the team steamrolled the archrival Yankees before undressing the Houston Astros, the defending champs who had toyed with them in the playoffs only 12 months earlier. Finally, they made quick work of the Dodgers, who had emerged as the National League's most dominant team in recent seasons.

Of course, it wasn't as easy as it may have appeared. The six-month-long regular season represents a grind, and the modern postseason format is similarly exhausting. That the Red Sox were so consistently dominant was a testament to not only their talent, but their mental toughness as well.

Still, it was difficult to digest what they had accomplished and wonder: Is this the same franchise that had so famously failed to win it all for so long?

In many ways, it was not.

PART 8

TRANSFORMATIVE FIGURES

22

Dick O'Connell

WHEN IT COMES TO CHAMPIONSHIP TROPHIES OR RINGS, Dick O'Connell's long stretch as general manager of the Red Sox might seem to have been a failure.

In the 21st century alone, after all, no fewer than three executives—Theo Epstein, Ben Cherington, and Dave Dombrowski—did what O'Connell could not: win a World Series for the Red Sox.

But O'Connell's tenure was remarkable in other ways, in a manner that can't as easily be shown in a trophy case.

He can claim credit for the 1967 American League championship team as architect of the first pennant in better than two decades for the organization. Further, he helped build contending teams that just missed out on the postseason in 1972 and 1974 before building a second pennant-winning team in 1975, that, like its predecessor, took a superior opponent to Game 7 of a classic World Series.

And even after he was forced out of his position in a bitter ownership battle that cleaved the club in half in the latter part of the 1970s, his fingerprints were all over the 1978 team, arguably the best Sox team to never qualify for the postseason.

It is not hyperbole to suggest that O'Connell's official elevation to the position of GM in 1965 was one of the most consequential hirings that Tom Yawkey ever facilitated.

To fully appreciate O'Connell's impact, you first have to understand how fallow a period of history preceded him.

For much of the 1950s until the mid-1960s, the Red Sox front office was a study in incompetence.

Under Joe Cronin, the Red Sox went nearly the entire decade of the 1950s with an all-white roster until they were shamed/pressured into integrating in 1959. From 1951 through the end of Cronin's reign in 1959, the Sox were the epitome of mediocrity, placing anywhere from third to sixth and never coming within single digits of the league leader in the American League standings.

When Ted Williams retired after 1960, things got exponentially worse. A sixth-place finish in 1961, the first year A.T. (After Ted) was, improbably, the team's *finest* until the 1967 turnaround. Even as a number of promising players began to emerge—including Carl Yastrzemski and Tony Conigliaro—the Red Sox were, at best, noncompetitive, and at worst, irrelevant.

O'Connell's history with the Red Sox dates back to 1949, when, fresh out of a career as Navy officer, he was hired to oversee a new minor league affiliate in Lynn, Massachusetts. From there, O'Connell worked his way up the organizational ladder, serving as director of park operations and sundry other front office titles.

("Pinky" Higgins owns the ignominious distinction of ranking among the team's worst executives *and* managers—for a time, doing both jobs poorly. He was a heavy drinker, which surely didn't help his job performance in either title, and also a known racist.)

When O'Connell was finally installed in the fall of 1965, the Red Sox began to turn the corner, both competitively and culturally.

On the field, the 1966 season was no better than the five or so years that preceded it. But O'Connell was having an impact, if for no other reason than he began to expand the organization's player pool to include a real commitment to Black and Latino players.

The 1966 roster featured a number of players of color, including future mainstays George Scott, Joe Foy, Reggie Smith, John Wyatt, Jose Tartabull, and Jose Santiago.

Said O'Connell of this philosophical shift: "I don't care what color a player is as long as he can play. If he is any good, I want to sign him."

This was no subtle shift on the part of the Red Sox. This was, instead, a complete about-face. Gone, almost overnight, was the Old Boy Network that had overseen a lily-white roster and decades of second-division baseball.

O'Connell had sent a clear message that it was a new era in Boston. For the past 15 or so seasons, an entire generation of Black stars—including Hank Aaron, Willie Mays, Bob Gibson, Frank Robinson, Willie McCovey, and Maury Wills—had transformed the industry in general and the game on the field, especially in the National League. And none, of course, would have been given a shot to play in Boston.

Another signature move of O'Connell's was the hiring of rookie manager Dick Williams, who replaced Billy Herman after the team had bottomed out in 1966, finishing second-to-last and, for the sixth straight season, failing to draw even a million fans.

Williams had managed the team's Triple A affiliate in Toronto to the International League pennant the previous season and was already familiar with many of the organization's top prospects in the minors.

But when O'Connell hired Williams, he wasn't as concerned with his manager's résumé or knowledge of its prospects. What O'Connell wanted was a sea change, and in Williams, he saw someone who could provide it.

"Williams was tough," O'Connell would tell the *Worcester Telegram* years later. "That's why I hired him. That's what we needed. The Red Sox always had managers who kissed their asses; I knew Williams would kick their asses."

Over the course of the Impossible Dream season of 1967, O'Connell made several shrewd pickups.

At the time, blockbuster in-season trades were not yet a thing. Baseball didn't have small-market teams looking to unload payroll at the midway point. Instead, trades were very much centered on talent alone, and O'Connell struck paydirt with a few.

Among the spare parts he obtained to help the Red Sox maneuver through the most competitive pennant race in more than a decade were utility man Jerry Adair, starter Gary Bell, and catcher Elston Howard, the latter of whom, though at the end of his career, had helped to guide several winning Yankee teams into October.

And finally, O'Connell made a small pickup that didn't pay much in the way of dividends that season, but would the next—outfielder Ken Harrelson, who was acquired in the wake of the horrific beaning suffered by Conigliaro in mid-August.

All of O'Connell's moves couldn't push the Sox to a title, as they lost out to the Cardinals over seven games. But his roster construction, his hiring of Williams, and his focus on scouting development represented the start of a new era for the Red Sox.

No longer would the Red Sox be lovable losers. No longer would they feature a homegrown lefty slugger...and little else. And no more would games be played in front of minuscule crowds.

It's hardly a stretch to suggest that, along with Yastrzemski and Williams, O'Connell played a sizable role in saving the Red Sox and turning them from laughingstock into perennial contender. The 1967 season was the first of 13 consecutive winning seasons.

* * *

As uplifting as the 1967 season had been, O'Connell's best work was still to come.

Working with farm director Neil Mahoney and a bevy of scouts, the Red Sox began to assemble a treasure trove of young, talented players. From 1967 through 1973, O'Connell oversaw the drafting and signing of Carlton Fisk, Cecil Cooper, Ben Oglivie, Bill Lee, Dwight Evans, Rick Burleson, Jim Rice, Butch Hobson, and Fred Lynn.

Fisk and Rice would be elected to the Hall of Fame, and Lynn might have been too, had he not been traded out of Boston in the years following O'Connell's ouster. Evans, arguably the greatest right fielder in the team's history, remains, as of this writing, a candidate for Cooperstown via the Veterans Committee.

In this era, it was critical for a team to be able to develop its own players. Free agency was still several years away, and teams were not able to simply purchase stars to fill holes on their roster. The amateur draft, meanwhile, had only been introduced in 1965, just as O'Connell was climbing the organizational ladder.

Even in a simpler era, O'Connell couldn't accomplish all he needed to do on his own. He required help, and he made strong hires for the scouting ranks and the player development side. Farm director Neil Mahoney helped build the infrastructure of the minor league system. Meanwhile, O'Connell hired and entrusted area scouts to make their recommendations about amateur players.

Their track record in this regard was almost unmatched, though a full accounting of their work in this period finds that they were far better at identifying position players and hitters than they were at uncovering pitchers.

But O'Connell's impact wasn't limited to the drafting and developing of players. In the era before the reserve clause was struck down and free agency was introduced, there were essentially two avenues of player procurement: the amateur draft and trades.

O'Connell was a master at the latter. With the team seemingly perennially in need of pitching, O'Connell dealt for what he had been unable to develop. In the span of a few seasons, O'Connell acquired Ray Culp, Sonny Siebert, Rick Wise, and Gary Peters. Of the collateral used to acquire that group, O'Connell would regret just one: outfielder Reggie Smith, who would go on to play another nine seasons in the National League and be named to the All-Star team five times.

His best move when it came to veteran pitching, however, was to sign Luis Tiant, who had been released twice in 1971—once by Minnesota and later by Atlanta.

Tiant's career in Boston began in a highly inauspicious fashion, as the Cuban with the whirling delivery and handlebar mustache lost seven of his first eight decisions and fashioned a bloated 4.85 ERA.

But starting in 1972, Tiant began a five-year stretch, at the age of 32, in which he could rightfully be called the best starting pitcher in the American League. In that span, Tiant was 96–58 with a 3.12 ERA, while averaging better than 260 innings and almost 20 complete games per season.

Not bad for a castoff on whom O'Connell had taken a chance.

The 1975 Red Sox—their lineup dotted with homegrown stars at three of the four infield positions, all three outfield spots, the DH, and behind the plate—were a force. They knocked off the three-time World Champion Oakland A's in an ALCS sweep before losing an epic World Series to the Cincinnati Reds.

Ironically, two of O'Connell's most noteworthy acquisitions would never appear in a game for the Sox.

In 1976, penurious A's owner Charlie Finley auctioned off some of his stars in an effort to remain financially solvent. While the rival Yankees picked up Vida Blue, who five years earlier had won both the AL MVP and Cy Young Awards, O'Connell bought reliever Rollie Fingers and outfielder Joe Rudi for $2 million.

Days later, commissioner Bowie Kuhn nullified all three transactions, claiming they ran counter to "the best interests of the game." While Rudi may have been a largely redundant addition to the roster, it's fascinating to consider what might have been had the Sox been able to retain Fingers, only the preeminent closer of his time and later elected to the Hall of Fame.

Had Fingers been part of, say, the 1978 team two years after his arrival, it's doubtful the Sox would have squandered the nine-game lead they held in mid-August in the first place.

Change, however, was coming to the Red Sox, and it wouldn't be good for O'Connell. While he was closely aligned with owner Tom Yawkey, who had saved his job in 1949, the same could not be said of his relationship with Yawkey's wife, Jean, with whom he barely spoke.

When Tom Yawkey died of cancer in July of 1976, just 10 months after his team nearly won the World Series, O'Connell almost immediately became a marked man. With Jean Yawkey, Haywood Sullivan, and Buddy LeRoux positioned to gain ownership of the club, Sullivan was summarily dismissed, effective immediately, in October of 1977.

In his final few seasons with the club, O'Connell continued to make some brilliant moves. Hall of Famer Wade Boggs was drafted on his watch, and the team took its first tentative steps into free agency, signing reliever Bill Campbell. It was hard not to view Campbell as anything other than a poor man's Fingers. Alas, his signing represented a classic "too little, too late" transaction.

O'Connell nearly enjoyed a triumphant return some six years later when LeRoux attempted an unsuccessful coup in 1983. But the effort was tossed out by the court system and O'Connell's second act never took place. It's fascinating to wonder about an alternate history of the Red Sox in which O'Connell was rehired and given the chance to remake the team in his image a second time.

(With the Red Sox and their ownership's dysfunction in full bloom, another pro team in town was not above leaning on O'Connell's expertise in team building. Boston Celtics president and GM Red Auerbach, who had known O'Connell for decades, hired him as a consultant in his later years.)

Still, over a period that saw him construct two different pennant-winning teams, reignite interest in baseball throughout

New England, and leave the organization in far better stead after his departure, O'Connell needed nothing further on his long list of achievements—except, of course, the championship that eluded him and every other coach, manager, executive, and owner who was associated with the team from 1919 through 2003.

The Red Sox franchise—and by extension, the Boston sports market—became so accustomed to winning in the 21st century that, at times, huge figures are somehow diminished because it wasn't their great good fortune to be associated with one of the teams that won it all.

But it would be difficult—if not impossible—to cite an executive other than Theo Epstein who had such a long-lasting, positive impact on the franchise as the man who disassociated it from its most troubling prejudices, executed a string of one-sided trades that benefited the club for years, built a remarkably consistent player development system, and ushered in an era that saw the Sox become permanently relevant—in their own city and throughout the game of baseball.

23

Theo Epstein

THE RED SOX HAVE A LONG TRADITION OF EMPLOYING general managers who were New England natives.

Dick O'Connell, Lou Gorman, Dan Duquette, Ben Cherington, Mike Hazen, and Brian O'Halloran all grew up in New England, every one of them Red Sox fans.

But no one grew up closer to Fenway than Theo Epstein, who, though born in New York, grew up in Brookline, Massachusetts, just several miles from the ballpark.

Epstein came to the job almost accidentally. When the John Henry–Tom Werner–Larry Lucchino ownership group was approved in 2002, spring training was already underway, and time was tight for making hirings.

Still, the new owners wanted a clean sweep from the past and dismissed both manager Joe Kerrigan and GM Dan Duquette. In Duquette's place, the team installed Mike Port as the interim GM for the year with a goal of undertaking a more thorough search of applicants after the 2002 season.

For a time—indeed, officially for a few fleeting hours—Billy Beane had an agreement with the Red Sox to leave the Oakland A's and become the Red Sox's president of baseball operations. At the time, Beane was seen as the leader of a new generation of executives who combined traditional player evaluation methods (scouting, etc.) with more revolutionary ones involving analytics.

Beane had found early success by searching for market inefficiencies and finding skill sets that had been underappreciated by other executives. Such an approach appealed to Henry in particular, who had become wildly successful in the field of hedge funds by employing a similarly advanced analytic approach.

But after weeks of back-and-forth negotiations for the Red Sox—first with Oakland ownership, and then Beane himself—Beane determined that he was unwilling to move from the Bay Area to the East Coast, even after the Sox had agreed to let him spend a significant period based in California to ease concerns about his family.

That prompted the Red Sox to start the search all over again. Before long, Epstein, who had spent the 2002 season as Port's assistant and was well known to Lucchino from their time together with the San Diego Padres, emerged as a candidate, despite his age (28) and relatively thin résumé.

Epstein's appointment to GM was greeted with mockery in some circles. A cartoon of Michael Jackson hanging Epstein off a balcony—as he had famously done in London with his own toddler—circulated and jokes were made about Epstein not being able to stay up late on school nights.

Epstein absorbed all the barbs about his youth and inexperience with good nature. But he—and the Red Sox—would have the last laugh.

Soon, it was clear how nontraditional Epstein would be. In a highly unorthodox move, Epstein claimed journeyman outfielder/first baseman Kevin Millar on waivers, blocking the Florida Marlins from selling Millar to a team in Japan. Such actions were unheard of at the time—teams simply didn't get in the way of a nearly completed transaction. But Epstein wasn't one to bow to convention.

In Millar, he saw a useful righty bat who could provide the Sox with an important piece. It didn't matter to him that the Marlins had other plans. This was hardball, and it was Epstein's charge to assemble the best roster available—the Old Boy Network be damned.

More moves followed, each designed to make the Red Sox better. How much better was almost incidental. Epstein saw the process of roster building as incremental, part of a puzzle. With each move, the pieces fit together a little better.

Circumstances, however, mandated more dramatic action after the 2003 season. The Red Sox lost Game 7 of the ALCS when Pedro Martinez faltered in the late innings and the Sox lacked a surefire closer option out of the bullpen.

For all the advances being made when it came to player evaluation, when the autopsy was performed on the 2003 Sox, even the most casual fan could see that the team had come up empty because of a lack of pitching.

There was no need to run programs through "Carmine," the Red Sox's computerized software system that was revealed in a lengthy *Sports Illustrated* feature; no need to consult with sabermetric godfather Bill James, or for any careful study of analytics. Simply put, the Red Sox, as had seemingly been the case for so many years in franchise history, needed arms.

That much was obvious to even the most casual observer. The 2003 Red Sox certainly didn't lack for offense, that's for sure. Those Sox had scored 961 runs, the second-most in franchise history, with six hitters contributing 20 or more homers and eight supplying 85 or more RBI.

So Epstein set out to address that obvious deficiency. He, along with assistant GM Jed Hoyer, spent Thanksgiving with Curt Schilling and his family in Arizona, attempting to persuade Schilling to waive a no-trade clause in his contract with the Arizona Diamondbacks.

With Schilling agreeable to a deal—and extended—the trade was made. It turned out to be a master stroke for Epstein, providing the Sox with another top-of-the-rotation starter.

The other was the signing of free agent Keith Foulke. The Red Sox loved that Foulke was durable beyond belief and capable of pitching more than one inning per outing. They would lean on Foulke heavily in the 2004 postseason—the team played 14 games that month and Foulke appeared in 11 of them, allowing a grand total of one earned run in 14 innings.

It was fitting that he was on the mound when the Sox finished off their sweep of the Cardinals for the first title in 86 years; a year earlier, the Red Sox didn't have a reliever of his dependability to whom they could turn late in postseason games.

But Epstein's boldest stroke—not only that season, but for his entire tenure in Boston—came at the trade deadline in the middle of the 2004 season.

The Red Sox were plodding along—in contention but underachieving somewhat in the American League playoff race.

Worse, the Sox weren't sure what they were going to get from shortstop Nomar Garciaparra.

Battling a variety of injuries, Garciaparra was in and out of the lineup in the first half, playing in just 38 of the first 100 games. He also sent a message to management that he was unsure how much he could be counted on in the second half of the season.

All of that proved too much for Epstein, who went into the trade deadline with a thought that would have been unthinkable only months earlier—to trade off Garciaparra.

Garciaparra had been a dynamic player for the Sox in his first seven seasons, winning two batting titles, scoring 100 or more runs on six occasions, and four times driving in 100 or more runs. In the mythical battle for Best Shortstop in the American League—a contest involving Derek Jeter, Alex Rodriguez, and Miguel Tejada—Garciaparra was the Boston entrant, and a homegrown one at that.

But Garciaparra's relationship with the team had begun to fray. Ownership had made a contract extension offer in the spring, but while Garciaparra deliberated, the offer was then pulled off the table. That, his uncertain availability, and, by extension, his deteriorating defensive play all conspired to force Epstein's hand.

In a stunning, complicated swap involving three other teams, Epstein dealt off Garciaparra and young outfielder Matt Murton and ended up with shortstop Orlando Cabrera and first baseman Doug Mientkiewicz.

It was audacious on Epstein's part, a point made patently obvious to him when he left Fenway after news of the deal became public and was met with expletive-filled rants from fans as he walked to nearby Kenmore Square.

That night, for the first time in his life, he took an Ambien to help him sleep.

The bold stroke proved to be just what the Red Sox needed—on the field and in the clubhouse. Cabrera brought dependability to the shortstop position, even if he wasn't nearly the offensive performer that his predecessor was. And, at first, the slick-fielding Mientkiewicz proved to be a huge upgrade.

Epstein had fretted that the team's shaky infield defense would be, in his words, his club's "fatal flaw," but that was now rectified.

At the same time, Garciaparra had become increasingly negative, a brooding presence in the clubhouse, warning teammates that management couldn't be trusted and railing against media coverage of the team. With Garciaparra gone, the mood lightened, and suddenly the atmosphere surrounding the Sox was instantly improved.

The real payoff came in October, when the team that Epstein had constructed rallied from what looked like certain defeat to the Yankees in the ALCS and then steamrolled the St. Louis Cardinals in four straight to capture their first championship in almost 90 years.

In a jubilant Red Sox clubhouse celebration, Epstein, who had a knack for saying the right thing at the right time, toasted the players and organization and proclaimed, "Now, 1918 is just another year in which the Red Sox won the World Series."

The room erupted in recognition. For years, the players, staff members and others in the organization had heard the cruel chants of "1918! 1918!" especially in New York. But the sweep of the Cardinals had disarmed that taunt and rendered it meaningless.

At the time, the analytics movement was in its infancy, and it was easy—if more than a little lazy—to suggest that Epstein was simply reacting to computer-generated data. But such a stance revealed ignorance.

It was never Epstein's intent to reinvent how players were evaluated; rather, he was looking to make the process more efficient and accurate. But while utilizing new data, Epstein never ran from the game's traditions.

Even as he expanded the way players were viewed and judged, he invested more into traditional methods. He hired additional scouts, hoping to blend both the old and new.

Nowhere was that more obvious than his reliance on someone like Bill Lajoie. Lajoie had been in the game since before Epstein was born, as a scout and front office official. He would later become GM of the Detroit Tigers before working with the Atlanta Braves and Milwaukee Brewers. Lajoie was as old-school as they came, and yet few held more sway with Epstein. If Lajoie endorsed a player, Epstein felt far more confident in signing or trading for him.

To Epstein, the wholesale changes going on in front offices weren't about discarding the old in favor of the new, but rather, blending the two.

"If you hire the best scouts," Epstein once said, "and put them in a position to see the player at the right time and get good, solid accurate scouting reports, you see the player through a strong traditional scouting lens. If you hire the best analysts, get the most accurate data, make the best adjustments, do the most thorough statistical information, that's another lens through which to view the player.

"The best way to see the player most accurately, to get the truest picture of the player, is to put those lenses together and look through them simultaneously."

Winning for the first time in 2004 was difficult enough. But defending that title proved to be a tall order. The Red Sox ultimately lost the division on a tiebreaker to the Yankees. Worse, the Sox had attempted to overtake the Yankees on the final weekend of the season, and in so doing, had scrambled their pitching plans for the postseason.

The team was summarily swept by the Chicago White Sox in the division series, a hugely disappointing end to the season. Things soon got worse.

A chasm had developed between Epstein and team president Larry Lucchino. The two had a history that dated back to their time together with the Baltimore Orioles, where Lucchino was a protégé of Orioles owner Edward Bennett Williams and Epstein was an intern.

When Lucchino became president of the San Diego Padres, he hired Epstein. While learning about scouting and player evaluation from Padres executive Kevin Towers, Lucchino had urged Epstein to get his law degree to better prepare him for his future in the game.

And when Lucchino was matched with Tom Werner and John Henry in a shotgun marriage arrangement to purchase the Sox in 2002, once again, Lucchino summoned Epstein to join him on his latest adventure.

But after three seasons as GM, Epstein began to chafe under Lucchino's direction. After three straight trips to the postseason, two ALCS appearances, and a world championship, Epstein believed he had the right to call his own shots in baseball operations. Lucchino, however, periodically weighed in, and, at times, cast a deciding vote on player personnel.

But this was less about autonomy and more about the direction of the franchise. Epstein's fear was that Lucchino was prioritizing branding over the on-field product.

Lucchino, meanwhile, was said to be envious of the credit that Epstein had gotten for the team's success.

With his contract expiring at the end of October, Epstein had, on a few occasions, privately speculated that it might be time to move on. Even when the Red Sox satisfied his contractual demands—lifting his salary from $350,000 annually to $1.5 million—there were bedrock philosophical issues that stood in the way of a return.

One night, after the 2005 postseason, I was driving home when my cell phone rang. The incoming number was blocked.

"Sean?" said a somewhat hushed and tremulous voice.

I recognized it immediately as John Henry.

"Hi John," I responded, unsure as to what I should owe this pleasure.

"Is Theo leaving?" asked Henry.

"I think so, yes," I responded.

"We've got to stop him!" exclaimed the only person who could accomplish such a feat, to a lowly sportswriter who had no such power.

As it turned out, there was no stopping Epstein. Dressed in a gorilla suit—which, at once, heightened the absurdity of the situation and provided him cover as he left Fenway Park—Epstein cleaned out his office and departed.

"In my time as general manager, I gave my entire heart and soul to the organization," said Epstein in a statement announcing his resignation. "During the process leading up to today's decision, I came to the conclusion that I can no longer do so."

And with that, the only baseball executive alive who could say he won a World Series for the Boston Red Sox was gone.

Epstein would spend much of the winter traveling with Pearl Jam throughout South America, allowing himself the kind of vacation that could never have been possible while working as a baseball executive.

In his absence, the Red Sox deployed a tandem that included Jed Hoyer and Ben Cherington—both of whom would go on to be successful executives—along with Jeremy Kapstein, a former agent with close ties to Lucchino.

Eventually, the Sox and Epstein resolved their differences and Epstein returned, having been granted assurance that the team would be more laser-focused than ever on matters on the field, and that he would enjoy independence from Lucchino, reporting directly to Henry.

The 2006 season, however, was a disaster. The Sox missed the postseason for the first time since 2002. But in the face of the disappointing season, Epstein remade the roster the following year, introducing homegrown players such as Dustin Pedroia, Jacoby Ellsbury, Jon Lester, and Clay Buchholz.

From the wreckage of the post-2005 walkout, Epstein had successfully built the core of the next great Red Sox team, one that captured the World Series in 2007.

In 2008, the Sox came much closer to successfully defending their first World Series title, going to a seventh game in the 2008 ALCS before bowing out to upstart Tampa Bay. Terry Francona, years later, would say that of all the teams he managed in Boston, the 2008 team may have been the most talented—a surprising declaration, given that two others had won titles.

But after 2008, the Sox began to backslide. They went from being swept out of the division series in 2009 to missing out on the playoffs altogether in 2010. And when the team squandered a huge lead in the wild-card race in the final month of 2011 and fell short of the postseason in a crazed, chaotic final night of the regular season, the writing was on the wall.

By then, Epstein had been with the Sox for a decade, nine of them as the GM. By his own admission, things had gotten stale, and it was time for a new challenge.

Within weeks of the Sox's final regular season game, Epstein had negotiated his own release from the Sox and become president of baseball operations with the Chicago Cubs.

He would meet with similar success there, bringing the Cubs—in many ways, the National League version of the Red Sox, without a championship for nearly a century—their own elusive title in 2016.

That one man could, in the span of a little more than a decade, end two droughts for franchises that felt similarly cursed, was testament to Epstein's creativity and management skills. It also all but ensures that he will someday be inducted into the Hall of Fame.

But it is his tenure with the Red Sox that will lead his legacy of achievements in baseball.

24
Terry Francona

THE BEST MANAGER IN RED SOX HISTORY WAS NOT EXACTLY a hot commodity when he was hired in December 2003.

Terry Francona had managed for four seasons in Philadelphia, without much distinction. His teams never sniffed a winning record—the closest he came was a 77-win season—and the Phillies were often out of contention by the All-Star break.

Naturally, this stretch of noncompetitive teams did not sit well with the Philly faithful. Francona had his car vandalized at Veterans Stadium. It was unclear whether the miscreants knew whose car they were damaging, but Francona, in later years, would jokingly maintain that they had indeed specifically targeted his ride.

(Even after his firing, Francona could be a target. When he returned as a scout for Cleveland a year after being dismissed,

Phillies team president Dave Montgomery assigned a security guard to stand watch near him for the entire series.)

Through his four seasons in Philadelphia, Francona never seemed to fit in with the locals. Sure, the win-loss record didn't help. But from the beginning, he was treated as an outsider, someone who didn't belong managing the local nine.

"My mentality didn't mesh there. I wasn't one of them and I wasn't comfortable," he said. "My personality in Philadelphia wasn't what they were looking for to begin with. And I wasn't an old Phillie."

When Francona was let go on the final day of the 2000 season, he had to take a few steps back when it came to baseball employment. He worked for Cleveland as a scout for a season, then served as a bench coach in Texas (2002) and Oakland (2003).

Along the way, he interviewed for a few managerial openings, but never got offered a job. So when Francona was interviewed for the Red Sox vacancy after the 2003 season, he was hardly the favorite. (Others interviewed at the time included Joe Maddon.)

But the Red Sox were coming off a season in which in-game strategy had become a sharp focus. The Sox had famously lost to the New York Yankees in the American League Championship Series, and in heartbreaking fashion. Manager Grady Little had chosen to stay with starter Pedro Martinez late in Game 7, to his detriment and regret. The Yankees rallied to tie the game off the great ace, then won in extra innings, and with it, the pennant.

It was as excruciating a loss as any in team history, and general manager Theo Epstein spent the offseason making sure that his team would not be short on pitching, obtaining starter Curt Schilling and reliever Keith Foulke.

No offseason transaction, however, turned out to be as important as finding Little's replacement.

At the time, the analytics revolution was just beginning to sprout in baseball, and the Sox took the opportunity to construct a computer simulation for Francona to "manage" as part of his job interview. His swift decision-making in that task helped convince Epstein and others of Francona's readiness.

The Sox were secure in the knowledge that Francona would make sound, strategic in-game decisions and wouldn't be averse to incorporating some of the statistical data to help him make those calls. (Little, at times, had disdain for the piles of statistical analysis presented to him by the front office, though he was smart enough to keep his displeasure to himself, pretending to incorporate the input, but mostly ignoring it.)

But ultimately, Francona succeeded in letting Epstein and the rest of the front office know that he could handle the demands of managing in Boston. This was a skill set that was not to be taken for granted.

There are other big-market franchises, subjected to intense media scrutiny and pressured by a demanding fan base—Philadelphia among them.

But in that era, with the Red Sox's title drought stretching toward a ninth decade, Boston was a challenge all its own. Coming ever-so-close, as the Red Sox had done the previous October, seemed to both heighten the expectations and harden the fans who had been conditioned for disappointment.

That fatalism, if not handled properly, could infect the team. The influence of talk radio was at an all-time high in the city, and players, coaches, and the manager couldn't escape its influence. Every game had become a referendum, every series a milestone by which the team would be judged.

Francona had already been exposed to the same phenomenon in Philadelphia, where the powerful WIP Radio—especially its acerbic morning show—had managed to grind players, coaches, and managers into pieces, worn down by the constant second-guessing and unrelenting criticism.

Francona had experienced this trial by fire and was expert at dismissing what Epstein would come to refer to as "the white noise."

He had something else, too. He had the experience of being a player—not a great one at the major league level, mind you, though he was enough of a standout at the University of Arizona to win the Golden Spikes Award, given annually to the best collegiate player in the nation. It was the baseball equivalent of the Heisman Trophy.

A first-round pick, Francona never enjoyed the same level of success in pro ball that he experienced in college, largely because of injuries. Francona tore up his knee early in his pro career and, by his own admission, was never the same afterward. His mobility on the bases and in the field was limited, and his balance and set-up at the plate were also negatively impacted.

Over the course of 10 major league seasons, he never had as many as 250 at-bats, utilized mostly as a platoon player or a bench option. In those 10 years, he played for five different franchises.

But while his playing career might have been unremarkable, Francona had benefited from a host of different experiences. He knew what it was like to be a high draft pick and the expectations that came with such status. Conversely, he knew what it was like to go into spring training fighting for a spot on the big-league roster.

Moreover, as a young boy, he spent summer vacations taking road trips with his father, John "Tito" Francona, who carved out a 14-year career in the big leagues. That exposure to big-league life as a grade schooler and later, a teenager, informed Francona's view of the game. He came to understand the traditions, the rhythm of a season, and the culture of the game.

Even before he went off to college, the younger Francona had an innate understanding of how major leaguers operated: how they prepared, what they thought, how they carried themselves. It gave him an incalculable head start.

Determining when to pull a pitcher or when to put the hit-and-run on were part of the everyday challenges for a big-league manager. But over the course of a season, those decisions had a way of evening out—some worked while others didn't.

But far more central to Francona's success was a simple credo: let players be themselves.

On the face of it, the credo seemed obvious. But Francona took the job in Boston just as the role of major league managers was undergoing a sea change.

For one thing, the era of the Dugout Hard-Ass—think Earl Weaver, or Billy Martin—was coming to a close. These managers were known for long, sometimes comical arguments with umpires and for ruling their clubhouse with absolute authority. Got a question for why a manager made a particular in-game decision, or why you weren't in the lineup? Best keep it to yourself, if you know what's good for you.

Francona had played for a variety of managers who were steeped in tradition and who ruled with absolute authority. Decisions were not up for debate and disciplinary measures were wielded. When Francona asked player-manager Pete Rose if he might return home for a day to attend the birth of his first child, Rose surprised him by answering in the affirmative.

He then quickly added the kicker: "...Just don't come back."

By the time Francona began his second major league managerial stint, things were changing in the game. Increasingly, players sought feedback and expected answers to their questions. Teams were no longer run with the authority of a military outfit. Suddenly, "Because I said so" wasn't a sufficient response.

Francona held firm to just a couple of rules: show up on time and play hard. Those guidelines hardly seemed restrictive or unreasonable.

Ironically, even as he became the model for the new, modern-day manager, Francona could, at times, look suspiciously like a throwback. He would habitually wrap bubble gum around a clump of chewing tobacco, then spit a river of ugly brown juice on the dugout floor for three hours.

Even allowing for Francona's loose ship, overseeing 25 different personalities represented a challenge. Martinez was fiercely proud and at times sensitive to public criticism, and it didn't take long for the ace and his new manager to clash.

In Francona's very first regular season game, a nationally televised game on Opening Night in Baltimore, Martinez pitched poorly and left Camden Yards before the game was over—a major violation of player protocol—thus avoiding any postgame questions from the Boston media.

It proved to be a huge flashpoint, right from the manager's first game. Reporters demanded to know whether Martinez's premature evacuation was a sign of disrespect toward a new manager, or evidence that the players were already running the show.

Francona was furious that Martinez had put him in a tough spot in his very first game, but quickly made the decision to deflect blame from Martinez and accept responsibility himself, explaining to the media that he had failed to inform his pitcher of team policy when it came to leaving the premises. It rang a bit hollow publicly—Martinez had been in the big leagues for a number of years by then and knew full well his actions were verboten—but in Francona's mind, enduring the skepticism was a far better outcome than having to publicly chastise such a key player on the roster.

This scenario would play out a number of times in Francona's tenure in Boston, and ultimately, it helped contribute to his exit. But more often than not, when confronted about a lapse in judgement by one of his star players—on or off the field—Francona invariably would cover for him, explaining it away as a mix-up in communication or a simple misunderstanding.

What the public—and oftentimes, the media—didn't know was that behind closed doors, players were very much held accountable for their actions. A reporter might ask Francona what he thought of, say, Manny Ramirez's refusal to run out a ground ball in the just-completed game, and the manager would skirt the issue or downplay it—minutes after Francona had brought Ramirez into his office and aired him out, out of sight and earshot of the media, for his lack of effort.

Francona understood the first rule of managing the modern athlete: never publicly embarrass him. But in the sanctity of the clubhouse, without the media's prying eyes or attentive ears, things were handled differently and the need for professionalism constantly preached.

The 2004 Red Sox were full of strong personalities, and Francona learned how and when to look the other way when they flouted convention.

"We try, as a team, to find an identity," Francona said. "The 2004 team was very loose. But when they got on the field, they cared about each other. And when the game started, they played the game the right way."

It may not have been standard behavior to perform naked pull-ups on the clubhouse door frame minutes before first pitch, but Johnny Damon didn't think so. It wasn't typical for teams to consume mini shots of Jack Daniels in the run-up to a playoff game, but that didn't stop Kevin Millar from offering them.

Francona mostly rolled—or sometimes averted—his eyes, engaged in some playful banter with the players, and went about preparing for the game, secure in the knowledge that for all their unorthodox habits when it came to dealing with stress, he would have their full commitment on the field.

In the 2004 postseason, it was precisely this loose, convention-flouting escapism that would allow them the proper frame of mind to mount the greatest comeback in the game's history.

After being embarrassed on their home field 19–8 in Game 3 of the epic ALCS showdown with the Yankees, the Red Sox were a strangely carefree bunch. Prior to Game 4, with their season perhaps just nine innings away from an ignominious end, Millar prowled the field and issued a battle cry.

Typically, players might resort to the hoariest of cliches at times like this. There would be talk of "backs against the wall" and vows to "take it one game at a time."

But these Red Sox were hardly typical.

"Don't let us win tonight," he warned, speaking *of* the Yankees, but *to* anyone who would listen. "Don't let us win tonight."

The Red Sox hadn't won a game in the series yet and were fresh off a nine-run drubbing the night before, but Millar had already played the rest of the series out in his head. "Then we've got Petey tomorrow and [Curt Schilling] in Game 6. And in a Game 7, anything can happen."

It was precisely this kind of unearned cockiness on which the Red Sox thrived that season—in part because they had a manager who wasn't going to police their every word or lecture them about such brashness.

Another key to Francona's success was his refusal to treat each of his players equally. Some, Francona did his best to avoid—frankly, communicating with them mostly via his bench coach and best friend, Brad Mills, his clubhouse consigliere. With others, however, he developed close bonds that transcended the manager-player dynamic.

It was hardly unusual to walk into the Red Sox clubhouse hours before gametime and see Francona, ensconced in his office, seated across the desk from a player, engaged in an epic game of cribbage. Sometimes, the visitor would be a prominent player like Dustin Pedroia, and the two would verbally spar as they played, hurling insults at one another.

(Had they wished to do so, Pedroia and Francona could have taken their act on the road and become a successful comedy duo. Their repartee was sharp, comical, and bracing, with neither holding back. To the uninitiated, Pedroia's shtick may have come off as disrespectful or even inappropriate. But when it mattered, Pedroia's respect for his manager was unquestioned and the manager had no better representative on the field when it counted.)

Other times, Francona seemed to bond with role players like backup catchers George Kottaras or Kevin Cash.

Francona was the ultimate creature of habit. Rare was the day that Francona wasn't already at the ballpark—home or away—before noon for a game that night. It was part of his daily routine, and he felt most comfortable being at the ballpark, to the point where not being there made him anxious. When the Red Sox visited Japan to start the 2007 season, the entire team traveling party was invited to a luncheon at the U.S. Embassy in Tokyo. After riding on the bus, seated next to his wife, Francona walked, shook the hands of a few dignitaries, and, after nervously and compulsively looking at his watch, excused himself from the proceedings—he simply had to get to the Tokyo Dome, with the start of that night's game just seven hours away.

In winning the 2004 World Series and ending, forever, the narrative that the Red Sox were doomed to always come up short, Francona acquired mythical status with New England baseball fans.

He escaped any blame when the team got bounced in the first round of the 2005 playoffs, and again in 2006 when the team managed to miss the playoffs for the first time since 2002.

By 2007, Epstein had largely remade the roster, providing Francona with a younger, more athletic group. Only a handful of players—Pedroia, Manny Ramirez, David Ortiz, Jason Varitek, Mike Timlin, Curt Schilling, and Tim Wakefield—were holdovers from the last team. Even as Epstein was demonstrating his ability to remake the team on the fly, Francona was demonstrating that he could win with a new bunch of players.

In 2008, the Red Sox came up just shy of their third trip to the World Series in the span of five years, losing to the Rays in a seven-game ALCS showdown. Francona later would say that, though it didn't win a pennant much less a title, the 2008 team was the most talented team of his eight-year stay in Boston.

From 2008, the regression began. In 2009 the team was unceremoniously swept in the Division Series by the Angels, and in 2010 missed out altogether for just the second time since Francona took over in the dugout.

It was 2011 when it all fell apart for Francona. He was going through a divorce, and his health wasn't great, making the long season even more trying. It appeared the Sox were going to get into the playoffs as the American League wild-card entry, with a nine-game lead in early September.

Then, it was as if the Sox forgot how to win, dropping 20 of their last 27 games. Nothing Francona tried worked. Even when it seemed like the Sox were going to claw back into the wild card with a big lead in Game No. 162, they blew it and lost in the ninth inning when Carl Crawford couldn't come up with a sinking liner in left field.

Literally minutes later, the Tampa Bay Rays completed a comeback win over the Yankees at Tropicana Field, and the Red Sox's season was done.

Days later, ownership informed Francona that it would not be bringing him back for 2012. Within weeks, there were leaked reports that Francona had lost control of the clubhouse, with players—mostly starting pitchers—consuming fried chicken and beer while the game was being played.

With two World Series wins to his credit and the unofficial title of most beloved manager in franchise history, Francona was sanguine about moving on. He never expected to stay in Boston his entire career.

"This place can age you a little bit," he concluded, reflecting on his tenure.

But in his eight seasons, the Red Sox did what they hadn't done in the previous 86 years—and they did it twice.

Acknowledgments

THERE'S AN ENDLESS LIST OF PEOPLE TO THANK FOR THE existence of this, my second book. Undoubtedly, I will have missed some. But, here goes.

I'll start where this book began, with Bill Ames of Triumph Books contacting me and making the offer and proposal. It sounded daunting at the outset; frankly, it was. But thanks to Bill for the offer.

I owe much to Michelle Bruton at Triumph, who offered guidance when things threatened to veer off-course and was unfailingly patient with me as events conspired to delay the completion of the book. Her encouragement along the way was indispensable.

Over the course of my career, I've been fortunate enough to work for a number of terrific sports editors, including Dave Reid, Dave Bloss, and Arthur Martone (all with the *Providence Journal*), Hank Hryniewicz and Mark Murphy (*Boston Herald*), Martone, again (Comcast SportsNet New England), and Greg Bedard (Boston Sports Journal). I learned great lessons from each of them and consider myself fortunate to have worked for them all.

A special thanks to Bill Ballou, who knows more about Red Sox history than anyone I know, and to Chris Cotillo, who helped with some suggestions. Pam Kenn, of the Red Sox, proved invaluable.

To the many fellow beat writers with whom I have shared countless press boxes, cab rides, and flights: thank you. There are too many to mention, but know that I value your friendship.

To my daughter, Liza; son, Conor; and stepdaughters, Amanda and Leah, thanks for your love and patience throughout all of this. To my grandson, Lucas, may this book serve as a survival tool while growing up in Yankee Country.

And finally, to my wife, Sue, who provided her customary love and support endlessly, while rescuing some chapters I feared lost due to my general technological ineptitude.

Appendix

Retired Numbers

1—Bobby Doerr; second baseman
4—Joe Cronin; shortstop, manager
6—Johnny Pesky; shortstop, third baseman
8—Carl Yastrzemski; left fielder, first baseman
9—Ted Williams; left fielder
14—Jim Rice; left fielder
26—Wade Boggs; third baseman
27—Carlton Fisk; catcher
34—David Ortiz; designated hitter, first baseman
42—Jackie Robinson*
45—Pedro Martinez; pitcher

** In 1997, the Red Sox joined MLB in retiring No. 42 in honor of Jackie Robinson.*

Red Sox in the National Baseball Hall of Fame

Luis Aparicio
Wade Boggs*
Lou Boudreau
Jesse Burkett
Orlando Cepeda
Jack Chesbro
Jimmy Collins*
Joe Cronin*

Andre Dawson
Bobby Doerr*
Dennis Eckersley
Rick Ferrell*
Carlton Fisk
Jimmie Foxx
Lefty Grove
Rickey Henderson
Harry Hooper*
Waite Hoyt
Ferguson Jenkins
George Kell
Heinie Manush
Juan Marichal
Pedro Martinez*
Herb Pennock
Tony Perez
Jim Rice*
Red Ruffing
Babe Ruth
Tom Seaver
Al Simmons
Lee Smith
John Smoltz
Tris Speaker
Dick Williams
Ted Williams*
Carl Yastrzemski*
Tom Yawkey*
Cy Young

**Hall of Fame lists Boston Red Sox as primary team*

Award-Winners

AL Most Valuable Player

1912: Tris Speaker, center fielder
1938: Jimmie Foxx, first baseman
1946: Ted Williams, left fielder
1949: Ted Williams
1958: Jackie Jensen, right fielder
1967: Carl Yastrzemski, left fielder
1975: Fred Lynn, center fielder
1978: Jim Rice, left fielder/designated hitter
1986: Roger Clemens, pitcher
1995: Mo Vaughn, first baseman
2008: Dustin Pedroia, second baseman
2018: Mookie Betts, outfielder

AL Cy Young Award

1967: Jim Lonborg
1986: Roger Clemens
1987: Roger Clemens
1991: Roger Clemens
1999: Pedro Martinez
2000: Pedro Martinez
2016: Rick Porcello

AL Rookie of the Year

1950: Walt Dropo, first baseman
1961: Don Schwall, pitcher
1972: Carlton Fisk, catcher
1975: Fred Lynn, center fielder
1997: Nomar Garciaparra, shortstop
2007: Dustin Pedroia, second baseman

AL Manager of the Year

1986: John McNamara
1999: Jimy Williams

Louisville Silver Slugger Award

Tony Armas, outfielder: 1984
Jason Bay, outfielder: 2009
Don Baylor, designated hitter: 1981
Adrian Beltre, third baseman: 2010
Mookie Betts, outfielder: 2016, 2018
Xander Bogaerts, shortstop: 2015–2016
Wade Boggs, third baseman: 1983, 1986–1989, 1991
Ellis Burks, outfielder: 1990
Rick Burleson, shortstop: 1981
Jacoby Ellsbury, outfielder: 2011

Dwight Evans, outfielder: 1981, 1987
Nomar Garciaparra, shortstop: 1997
Adrian Gonzalez, first baseman: 2011
Mike Greenwell, outfielder: 1988
Carney Lansford, third baseman: 1981
J.D. Martinez, outfielder, designated hitter: 2018
Bill Mueller, third baseman: 2003
David Ortiz, designated hitter: 2004–2007, 2011, 2013, 2016
Dustin Pedroia, second baseman: 2008
Manny Ramirez, outfielder: 2001–2006
Jim Rice, outfielder: 1983–1984
John Valentin, shortstop: 1995
Jason Varitek, catcher: 2005
Mo Vaughn, first baseman: 1995

Rawlings Gold Glove Award

Mookie Betts, outfielder: 2016–2018
Mike Boddicker, pitcher: 1990
Jackie Bradley Jr., outfielder: 2018
Ellis Burks, outfielder: 1990
Rick Burleson, shortstop: 1979
Jacoby Ellsbury, outfielder: 2011
Dwight Evans, outfielder: 1976, 1978–1979, 1981–1985
Carlton Fisk, catcher: 1972
Adrian Gonzalez, first baseman: 2011
Doug Griffin, second baseman: 1972
Jackie Jensen, outfielder: 1959
Ian Kinsler, second baseman: 2018
Fred Lynn, outfielder: 1975, 1978–1980
Frank Malzone, third baseman: 1957–1959
Dustin Pedroia, second baseman: 2008, 2011, 2013–2014
Tony Pena, catcher: 1991

Jim Piersall, outfielder: 1958
George Scott, first baseman: 1967–1968, 1971
Reggie Smith, outfielder: 1968
Jason Varitek, catcher: 2005
Shane Victorino, outfielder: 2013
Carl Yastrzemski, outfielder: 1963, 1965, 1968–1969, 1971, 1976–1977
Kevin Youkilis, first baseman: 2007

Wilson Defensive Player of the Year Award
2012: Dustin Pedroia
2013: Dustin Pedroia
2016: Dustin Pedroia (second base), Mookie Betts (outfield)
2018: Mookie Betts (outfield)

Overall Winner
2013: Dustin Pedroia (American League)
2016: Mookie Betts (MLB)

AL Hank Aaron Award
2004: Manny Ramirez, outfielder
2005: David Ortiz, first baseman/designated hitter
2008: Kevin Youkilis, first baseman/third baseman
2016: David Ortiz
2018: J.D. Martinez, outfielder/designated hitter

Mariano Rivera AL Reliever of the Year Award
1977: Bill Campbell
1998: Tom Gordon
2017: Craig Kimbrel (AL)

Comeback Player of the Year Award

2011: Jacoby Ellsbury
2016: Rick Porcello

Edgar Martinez Outstanding Designated Hitter Award

1973: Orlando Cepeda
1975: Jim Rice
1986: Don Baylor
2003: David Ortiz
2004: David Ortiz
2005: David Ortiz
2006: David Ortiz
2007: David Ortiz
2011: David Ortiz
2013: David Ortiz
2016: David Ortiz

Roberto Clemente Award

2010: Tim Wakefield
2011: David Ortiz

Babe Ruth Award

2004: Keith Foulke
2007: Jonathan Papelbon
2013: David Ortiz
2018: David Price

MLBPAA Heart and Hustle Award

2013: Dustin Pedroia
2018: Mookie Betts

All-MLB Team

2019: Xander Bogaerts, shortstop, first team
Mookie Betts, outfielder, second team

Baseball America *Manager of the Year*

1999: Jimy Williams
2007: Terry Francona

Sporting News *Manager of the Year Award*

1967: Dick Williams
1975: Darrell Johnson
1986: John McNamara
1999: Jimy Williams
2013: John Farrell

Associated Press Manager of the Year Award

1967: Dick Williams
1975: Darrell Johnson

Sporting News *Executive of the Decade (2009)*

Theo Epstein

Sports Illustrated *Best General Manager of the Decade (2009)*

Theo Epstein

Baseball America *Major League Executive of the Year*

2008: Theo Epstein

Associated Press Athlete of the Year

1957: Ted Williams
1967: Carl Yastrzemski
1975: Fred Lynn

Triple Crown Champions

Batting

1942: Ted Williams (.356, 36, 137)

1947: Ted Williams (.343, 32, 114)

1967: Carl Yastrzemski (.326, 44, 121)

Pitching

1901: Cy Young (33, 158, 1.62)

1999: Pedro Martinez (23, 313, 2.07)

Postseason and All-Star Game MVP Award

World Series MVP

2004: Manny Ramírez

2007: Mike Lowell

2013: David Ortiz

2018: Steve Pearce

Lee MacPhail MVP Award (ALCS)

1986: Marty Barrett

2004: David Ortiz

2007: Josh Beckett

2013: Koji Uehara

2018: Jackie Bradley Jr.

*All-Star Game MVP**

1970: Carl Yastrzemski

1986: Roger Clemens

1999: Pedro Martinez

2008: J.D. Drew

**Renamed Ted Williams Most Valuable Player Award in 2002*

Team Captains

Doc Gessler (1909)
Harry Hooper (1918–20)
Everett Scott (1921)
Carl Yastrzemski (1966, 1969–83)
Jim Rice (1985–89)
Jason Varitek (2005–11)

Single-Season Leaders

Hitters

Batting Champions

1938: Jimmie Foxx (.349)
1941: Ted Williams (.406)
1942: Ted Williams (.356)
1947: Ted Williams (.343)
1948: Ted Williams (.369)
1950: Billy Goodman (.354)
1957: Ted Williams (.388)
1958: Ted Williams (.328)
1960: Pete Runnels (.320)
1962: Pete Runnels (.326)
1963: Carl Yastrzemski (.321)
1967: Carl Yastrzemski (.326)
1968: Carl Yastrzemski (.301)
1979: Fred Lynn (.333)
1981: Carney Lansford (.336)
1983: Wade Boggs (.361)
1985: Wade Boggs (.368)
1986: Wade Boggs (.357)
1987: Wade Boggs (.363)
1988: Wade Boggs (.366)
1999: Nomar Garciaparra (.357)
2000: Nomar Garciaparra (.372)
2002: Manny Ramírez (.349)
2003: Bill Mueller (.326)
2018: Mookie Betts (.346)

Home Run Champions

1910: Jake Stahl (10)
1918: Babe Ruth (11)
1919: Babe Ruth (29)
1939: Jimmie Foxx (35)
1941: Ted Williams (37)
1942: Ted Williams (36)
1947: Ted Williams (32)
1949: Ted Williams (43)
1965: Tony Conigliaro (32)
1967: Carl Yastrzemski (44)
1977: Jim Rice (39)
1978: Jim Rice (46)

1981: Dwight Evans (22)
1983: Jim Rice (39)
1984: Tony Armas (43)
2004: Manny Ramírez (43)
2006: David Ortiz (54)

RBI Champions
1902: Buck Freeman (121)
1903: Buck Freeman (104)
1919: Babe Ruth (114)
1938: Jimmie Foxx (175)
1939: Ted Williams (145)
1942: Ted Williams (137)
1947: Ted Williams (114)
1949: Vern Stephens and Ted Williams (159)
1950: Walt Dropo and Vern Stephens (144)
1955: Jackie Jensen (116)
1958: Jackie Jensen (122)
1959: Jackie Jensen (112)
1963: Dick Stuart (118)
1967: Carl Yastrzemski (121)
1968: Ken Harrelson (109)
1978: Jim Rice (139)
1983: Jim Rice (126)
1984: Tony Armas (123)
1995: Mo Vaughn (126)
2005: David Ortiz (148)
2006: David Ortiz (137)
2016: David Ortiz (127)
2018: J.D. Martinez (130)

Pitchers

Winning Games Leaders

1901: Cy Young (33)
1902: Cy Young (32)
1903: Cy Young (28)
1912: Smoky Joe Wood (34)
1935: Wes Ferrell (25)
1942: Tex Hughson (22)
1955: Frank Sullivan (18)
1967: Jim Lonborg (22)
1986: Roger Clemens (24)
1987: Roger Clemens (20)
1999: Pedro Martinez (23)
2004: Curt Schilling (21)
2007: Josh Beckett (20)
2016: Rick Porcello (22)

Strikeouts Leaders

1901: Cy Young (158)
1942: Tex Hughson (113)
1967: Jim Lonborg (246)
1988: Roger Clemens (291)
1991: Roger Clemens (241)
1996: Roger Clemens (257)
1999: Pedro Martinez (313)
2000: Pedro Martinez (284)
2001: Hideo Nomo (220)
2002: Pedro Martinez (239)
2017: Chris Sale (308)

ERA Leaders

1901: Cy Young (1.62)
1914: Dutch Leonard (0.96)
1915: Smoky Joe Wood (1.49)
1916: Babe Ruth (1.75)
1935: Lefty Grove (2.70)
1936: Lefty Grove (2.81)
1938: Lefty Grove (3.08)
1939: Lefty Grove (2.54)
1949: Mel Parnell (2.78)
1972: Luis Tiant (1.91)
1986: Roger Clemens (2.48)
1990: Roger Clemens (1.93)
1991: Roger Clemens (2.62)
1992: Roger Clemens (2.41)
1999: Pedro Martinez (2.07)
2000: Pedro Martinez (1.74)
2002: Pedro Martinez (2.26)
2003: Pedro Martinez (2.22)